HAMPS
& THE NEW
FOREST

YEAR ROUND WALKS

Spring, Summer, Autumn & Winter

Vicky Fletcher

COUNTRYSIDE BOOKS
NEWBURY BERKSHIRE

First published 2018

COUNTRYSIDE BOOKS
3 Catherine Road
Newbury
Berkshire

To view our complete range of books please visit us at
www.countrysidebooks.co.uk

ISBN 978 1 84674 361 0

Photographs by Vicky Fletcher

Produced by The Letterworks Ltd., Reading
Typeset by KT Designs, St Helens
Printed by Holywell Press, Oxford

Contents

Introduction

Spring

1 **Durley** .... *Spring* 7
3 miles / 4.8km

2 **Hurstbourne Tarrant** .... *Spring* 11
3.75 miles / 6km

3 **Boldre and Roydon Woods** .... *Spring* 15
4.25 miles / 6.8km

4 **Broughton Down** .... *Spring* 20
5.25 miles / 8.4km

5 **Beacon Hill** .... *Spring* 24
6.25 miles / 10km

Summer

6 **Southwick** .... *Summer* ... 28
5 miles / 8km

7 **River Hamble and Holly Hill Woodland Park** .... *Summer* ... 33
2.75 miles / 4.4km

8 **Preston Candover** .... *Summer* ... 37
4.25 miles / 6.8km

9 **Ibsley and Rockford Commons** .... *Summer* 41
4 miles / 6.4km

10 **Hartley Wintney and Hazeley Heath** .... *Summer* ... 46
4.5 miles / 7.2km

Contents

Autumn

11 **Compton** .... *Autumn* 51
5 miles / 8km

12 **Hinton Ampner and Kilmeston** .... *Autumn* ... 55
4.5 miles / 7.2km

13 **Rhinefield** .... *Autumn* .. 59
2 miles / 3.2km

14 **East Worldham** .... *Autumn* ... 63
4 miles / 6.4km

15 **Netley Abbey and Royal Victoria Country Park** .... *Autumn* .. 68
2 or 4.5 miles / 3.2 or 7.2km

Winter

16 **Emsworth Harbour** .... *Winter* 73
4 miles / 6.4km

17 **Kingsclere and Watership Down** .... *Winter* 77
4 miles / 6.4km

18 **Chalton Down and St Hubert's Church** .... *Winter* 82
5.5 miles / 8.8km

19 **Overton** .... *Winter* 87
5 miles / 8km

20 **Burley and the Holmsley Railway Line** .... *Winter* 92
3.5 miles / 5.6km

Introduction

Hampshire is a beautiful county, with lovely walks at any time of the year. There is a wide variety of countryside from the South Downs to the New Forest, the South Hampshire coast to the chalk hills of the North Wessex Downs

When faced with a grey February day or a cold, wet spring though, sometimes it is very hard to find the motivation to get out. That is where this book comes in. I have picked out 20 lovely walks from around the county that are great all year round, but with particular points of interest in different seasons to help tempt you out throughout the year. There are walks where you will see stunning spring bluebells, heathlands in bloom in late summer, glorious autumn colours in woodlands and uplifting winter walks with a warm pub to welcome you on your return. The walks range from 2 miles to 6 miles, so can be attempted by everyone and not just the super fit. I have mentioned where walks are particularly family friendly. Several are accessible by train or public transport.

Walking is being increasingly promoted by the NHS to help us all keep fit and healthy not just physically but also in terms of mental health. Walking is a great way to boost your mood and reduce stress and anxiety. That will come as no surprise to those who have been walking for years!

My favourite walks involve beautiful views, but I also love looking out for wildlife on walks. Seeing the countryside change over the year gives me a sense of connection to the outside world. A nice walk also really helps put the stresses and strains of life into perspective.

I hope you enjoy the walks as much as I have enjoyed finding them.

Vicky Fletcher

Acknowledgements

Many thanks to my husband Rob Gazzard and my mum Anne Fletcher for their company on many of these walks, and also our dog Darcy.

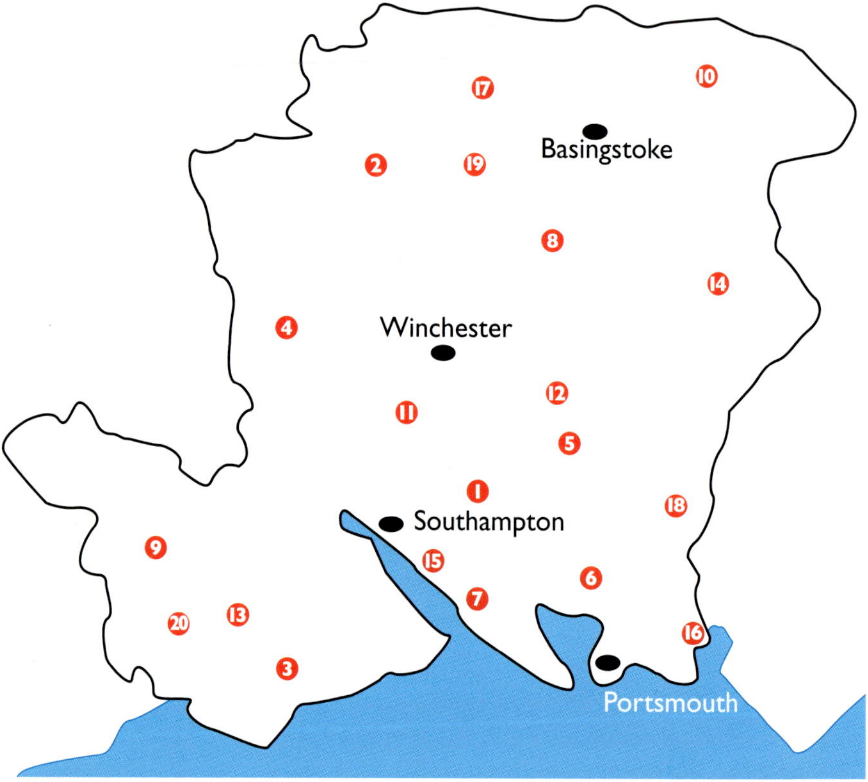

PUBLISHER'S NOTE

We hope that you obtain considerable enjoyment from this book; great care has been taken in its preparation. In order to assist in navigation to the start point of the walk, we have included the nearest postcode, although of course a postcode cannot always deliver you to a precise starting point, especially in rural areas. Although at the time of publication all routes followed public rights of way or permitted paths, diversion orders can be made and permissions withdrawn.

We cannot, of course, be held responsible for such diversion orders or any inaccuracies in the text which result from these or any other changes to the routes, nor any damage which might result from walkers trespassing on private property. We are anxious, though, that all the details covering the walks are kept up to date, and would therefore welcome information from readers which would be relevant to future editions.

The simple sketch maps that accompany the walks in this book are based on notes made by the author whilst surveying the routes on the ground. They are designed to show you how to reach the start and to point out the main features of the overall circuit, and they contain a progression of numbers that relate to the paragraphs of the text.

However, for the benefit of a proper map, we do recommend that you purchase the relevant Ordnance Survey sheet covering your walk. Ordnance Survey maps are widely available, especially through booksellers and local newsagents.

Walking through the beautiful bluebell wood.

1 Durley

3 miles / 4.8km

Just minutes from busy Southampton and Hedge End, the village of Durley feels like worlds away. This short walk in easy terrain is an ideal walk to tempt you back outdoors in spring. The walk weaves through pretty village lanes and peaceful farmland filled with birdsong and has views across the upper River Hamble valley. Stretches of woodland on the walk are filled with stunning arrays of bluebells and other spring flowers in April. Along the route lies an old mill which used the power of the River Hamble to mill flour in the 18th and 19th centuries. The walk starts and finishes at a popular traditional village pub.

The Walk

1 From the **Farmers Home** turn right into **Heathen Street**, a quiet village road. Continue for 500m or so past houses, a public footpath on your left (you will return from here later) and another lane on the left. Opposite **Stapleford Lane** on the right, look out for a double metal gate on the left in the hedge and a stile.

The Facts

Terrain A gentle landscape mostly along well-surfaced paths, although can be muddy in places particularly within fields in the last section of the walk. Over 10 stiles.

Map OS Explorer OL 3 Meon Valley.

Starting point Car park at the Farmers Home pub (GR SU 515161).

How to get there & parking Durley is located between the B3354 to the north of Hedge End and the B3035 west from Bishop's Waltham. The Farmers Home is signposted from Durley Street, turning down Parsonage Lane. Do ask permission before parking. **Sat nav** SO32 2BT.

Refreshments The Farmers Home, Durley. ☎ 01489 860457 www.thefarmers-home.co.uk.

2 Cross the stile into a meadow and continue straight on towards the woodland shelter belt. Go over a small footbridge crossing a ditch and continue up a slight incline. The path soon becomes a farm track with a hedge to the right and views over the fields to the left. Skirt **Hill Farm** with a sharp right-then-left turn, and continue straight on through open fields.

Sheep on farmland passed on the walk.

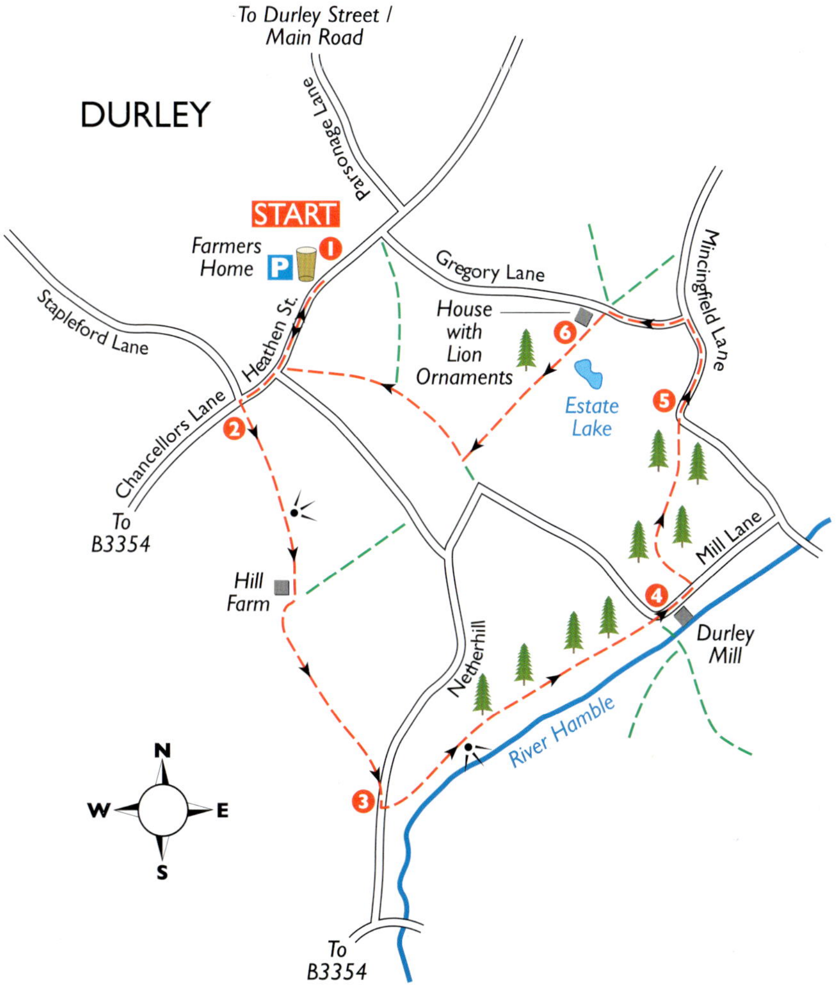

3 On reaching **Netherhill** turn right along the road and continue for a few metres. Look out for a stile and footpath sign in the hedge to your left just before the driveway of a large house. Cross the stile into fields with a hedge to the right-hand side at first, then opening up to give views across the upper **River Hamble valley** (a mere stream here compared to the wide estuary it becomes in Walk 7). Continue straight on through fields, crossing three stiles before reaching a short stretch of pathway with wooded valley sides and beautiful displays of bluebells and other spring flowers in April. A kissing gate at the end of the wooded stretch leads to **Mill Lane**.

4 Turn right here and pass **Durley Mill**, a former watermill used to process wheat into flour and now a Grade II listed building. A few metres further on, turn left down a driveway and take the footpath on your right-hand side leading between horse paddocks. The footpath then turns slightly to the left, then right, passing down into another shallow wooded valley, again enjoying the woodland flowers on display.

5 On emerging into **Mincingfield Lane** turn left and left again into **Gregory Lane**. Pass a postbox and, after a few metres, look out for a wooden fence and stile on the left before two large houses ahead of you (the first sporting two rather impressive gate-lions).

6 Crossing the stile into fields and a small lake to the left, continue straight on. Towards the end of the garden boundary, cross a stile into a small copse and then into arable fields. Continue straight on, keeping the field boundary to the left-hand side. At a large metal gate where a track joins from the left, cross the stile and turn right walking downhill now with a large arable field on your left and the field boundary to your right. Follow this footpath all the way back to **Heathen Street**, crossing a small stream at the bottom of the field to the road. Turn right and continue back to the Farmers Home.

What to look out for –

Spring flowers

The woodland stretches of this walk are filled with stunning arrays of spring flowers, including bluebells, white wood anemones and yellow lesser celandine. These delicate spring flowers are able to take advantage of the lengthening spring days, milder weather and increased light levels available in April down on the woodland floor before the trees are fully in leaf and stop so much sunlight reaching the ground level.

The stunning views over Hurstbourne Tarrant on a fine spring day.

spring

2 Hurstbourne Tarrant

3.75 miles / 6km

With lambs in the fields, bluebell woodlands, great views and beautiful historic buildings, this walk has many points of interest in spring. On the southern edge of the North Wessex Downs Area of Outstanding Natural Beauty, Hurstbourne Tarrant nestles amongst gentle hills in this picturesque chalk downland landscape. After admiring the 12th-century church, the route passes along the valley of the Bourne Rivulet, a winterbourne and tributary of the River Test, to Ibthorpe House with connections to Jane Austen. A moderate ascent brings rewarding views over the hills towards distant Andover. After walking through ancient woodland with carpets of bluebells and other spring flowers, you emerge back into the rolling farmland with views along the Bourne Valley.

The Walk

1 From the recreation ground car park, turn left along the lane back to the main road (B3048). Cross to **St Peter's Church** opposite.

2 Walk around the church to the northwest corner of the churchyard and cross via a stile into a small orchard with the ancient wall of **Parsonage Farm** to your left-hand side. Cross another stile into a grassy field and continue straight

spring

The Facts

Terrain An undulating landscape, mostly along flat paths but with a moderate climb and descent. Paths can be muddy within the woodland sections.

Map OS Explorer 131 Romsey, Andover & Test Valley.

Starting point Car park at the community centre and recreation ground in Hurstbourne Tarrant (GR SU 385528).

How to get there & parking Hurstbourne Tarrant is 4 miles north of Andover on the A343. Turn southeast onto the B3048 towards Stoke and St Mary Bourne then turn right after the school for the Community Centre car park. **Sat nav** SP11 0AX.

Refreshments The George and Dragon Inn ☎ 01264 736277 www.georgeanddragon.com or the Tea Cosy tea shop ☎ 01264 736644.

on towards a kissing gate. The path skirts along the back of houses in the village with glimpses of the downs behind.

3 The path emerges between houses onto the A343. Taking care, cross this busy road and continue straight on along the path opposite, between a house and a hedge. Cross through a kissing gate and two further gates into a horse

Parts of St Peter's church date back to the 12th century.

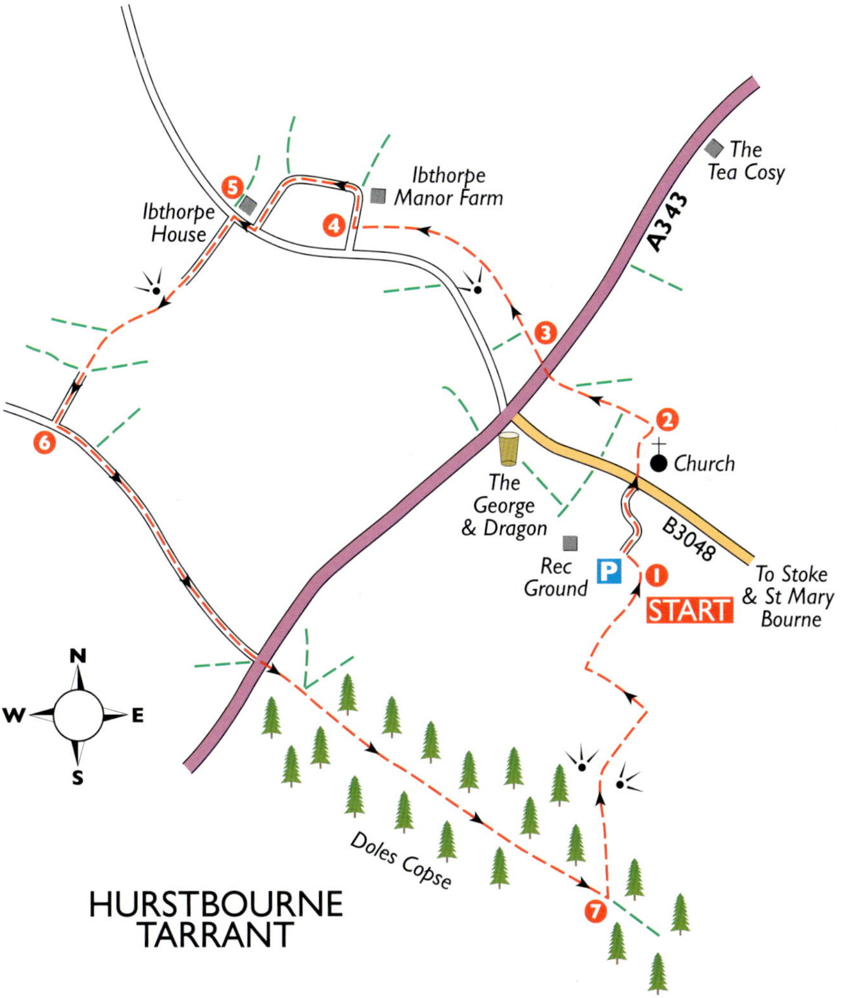

paddock and through a further kissing gate. Keeping to the path through this open countryside, enjoy views across the valley bottom to **Ibthorpe Manor Farm**.

4 At a gate emerging onto the driveway of the house, turn left and follow the driveway round to the right. Pass through a gate onto **Horseshoe Lane**. Turn right along the lane through the hamlet of **Ibthorpe**, with its lovely thatched cottages, to a small green at the junction with **Vernham Street**. **Ibthorpe Manor** is the Georgian house on the right-hand side.

5 Turn right along the road, over a bridge, and turn left onto **Windmill Hill** ready for a moderate climb. The tarmac road passes thatched cottages before it turns into a green lane.

6 At the top of the hill, pause to admire views south towards Andover before turning left along the road. At a junction with the A343, cross the road and continue straight on along a pathway between hedges and fields, which soon passes into **Doles Copse**. Continue through the woodland for three quarters of a mile, ignoring the first signposted path to the left.

7 At a boundary between deciduous and coniferous woodlands, turn sharp left waymarked **Test Way**. Descend through the woodlands back into the farmed chalk downland, enjoying views along the valley. Continue downhill between two fields, turn left at the bottom of the field, then right at a large barn back to the recreation ground and car park.

What to look out for –

Ibthorpe House

Not to be confused with Ibthorpe Manor Farm, Ibthorpe House is a handsome Georgian house on Horseshoe Lane. The house was visited regularly by Jane Austen and her sister Cassandra to visit and stay with close friends, the Lloyd family. Jane grew up in Steventon, around 10 miles away. The Lloyds had once been tenants of the Austens and Mary and Martha Lloyd became good friends with Jane and Cassandra. Mary Lloyd later married Jane's brother, James Austen in Hurstbourne Tarrant in 1796.

The pathway from Haywards Farm to Roydon Woods.

3 Boldre and Roydon Woods

4.25 miles / 6.8km

This walk starts near Boldre, towards the southern edge of the New Forest National Park and passes through a wide variety of beautiful countryside. In the first section you will be walking beside the Lymington River for a short stretch before passing the Church of St John the Baptist with two interesting historical associations. You then pass into Roydon Woods nature reserve and Site of Special Scientific Interest. Paths through the reserve pass first through bluebell woodlands and then out into open heathland, alive with blazing yellow gorse in springtime before returning through farmland.

The Walk

1 Walk south from the car parking point down **Royden Lane**, with **Church Lane** on your left-hand side and **Sandy Down** lane to your right. The lane is soon joined from the right by **Lower Sandy Down**, crosses a stream and,

The Facts

Terrain Undulating with some gentle climbs and descents; mainly on tracks, lanes and good paths but can be muddy in places after rain.

Map OS Explorer OL 22 New Forest.

Starting point Royden Lane (GR SZ 318994).

How to get there & parking Boldre is just off the A337 between Brockenhurst and Lyndhurst, signposted to 'Sandy Down and Boldre Church' and follow this road down to the junction with Royden Lane. On-road parking on the corner of Royden Lane, Church Lane and Sandy Down. Alternative parking at St John's Church, or the corner of Thistle Lane and Church Lane. **Sat nav** SO41 8PJ.

Refreshments The Red Lion in Boldre ☎ 01590 673177 www.redlionboldre.co.uk, The Hobler ☎ 01590 623944 www.thehobler.co.uk, or The Filly Inn on the A337 ☎ 01590 623449 www.thefillyinn.co.uk.

shortly after this, look out for a footpath sign in the hedge on your left-hand side opposite **Tidebrook Lodge**. Pass through a kissing gate and cross the common to a stile in the opposite corner of the field, now walking alongside the **Lymington River** on your left-hand side.

The river is a Site of Special Scientific Interest. Watch out for the rare summer snowflake flower along the route.

At a metal gate, cross the stile into a pasture field, still alongside the river. Cross a footbridge over the river and continue along the path past a water works. Turn right down a concrete drive.

2 At **Rodlease Lane** turn left, and right at a plant nursery following the footpath sign up a wooded track. Emerging into **Church Lane** with a wide gravel drive opposite (**Thistle Lane**), turn left up Church Lane to the **Church of St John the Baptist**. After taking time to explore the church (see box), walk towards the back of the churchyard. Cross the car park to a footpath, and continue between the fields to **Haywards Farm** to join **Thistle Lane**. Turn left down this gravel lane, and continue for just under half a mile to a fork in the path.

The very fine Haywards Farm is a Grade II listed building – look out for the old boarded barn on staddle stones, typical of old grain stores in Hampshire.

3 Take the left-hand lane, past **Dilton Gardens**, and soon you reach the Hampshire and Isle of Wight Wildlife Trust nature reserve, **Roydon Woods**.

Boldre and Roydon Woods

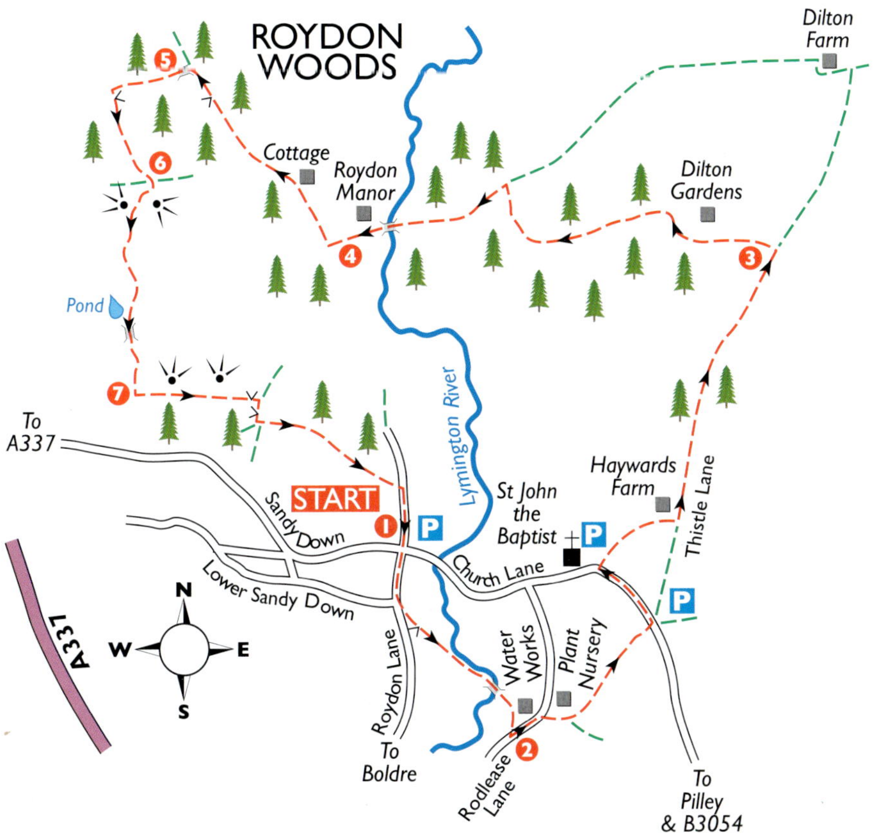

The gravel lane turns into a wide track through the woods. Continue through the woods on this track for around 500m until you reach a distinct T-junction of paths in the wood signposted for **Dilton** (right) and **Brockenhurst** (left). Turn left, walking downhill to a footbridge and crossing Lymington River again. There are views here of **Roydon Manor**, a 17th-century Grade II listed building. Continue straight on for a few hundred metres until you reach another T-junction of paths.

4 Turn right down a concrete drive. Walking slightly uphill now, the track passes a charming forester's cottage in the woods. At a fork in the paths, take the right-hand fork, leaving the wide gravel path and continuing up the rise with views of farmland on the right and woodland on the left. The path dips downhill. Pass through a gate, and across a small stream. The path continues

Dogs and walkers enjoying Lymington River in Roydon Woods.

back uphill. Look out for a small footbridge on the left, and cross into the woodland.

5 Now, following red and white waymarkers, the path runs along a boundary ditch to the left, marked with large trees. Pass through a holly copse. At a fork of paths take the left-hand fork still following the red and white waymarkers. The path goes down into a dip, following a post and wire fence on the right. Pass through a kissing gate, over a small footbridge across a ditch, and back up the other side of the dip, into more open grassy birch woodland. Continue through a further kissing gate.

6 On reaching a gravel path, turn left and immediately take the permissive path on the right, following pale blue and yellow waymarkers. Follow a rutted track initially through pine woodland and then out into open heathland. Keep to the path down into the valley, passing a small pond on your right. Cross a small bridge over a small stream, and walk back up the other side of the valley through open heathland. At a small fork of paths, take the right-hand fork, still following the yellow and blue waymarkers.

7 At the top of the valley, at a junction of paths turn left, now with views over the valley to the left, and occasional views of properties through pine woodland to your right. Continue along this ridge still following pale blue markers until you reach a gate. Turn right, away from the heath. Turn left after a wooden gate with a kissing gate. With fields to your right and woodland on your left, follow this path down through the wooded path to another kissing gate and onto Royden Lane. Turn right along the lane to reach your car.

What to look out for –

St John the Baptist Church

The churchyard is the final resting place for the Reverend William Gilpin, an 18th-century social reformer and also known for his written works on 'the picturesque', which influenced artistic tastes in landscape painting for generations, and encouraged a growing trend of travelling for leisure in the UK to go and see beautiful places. There is also a moving memorial to HMS *Hood* and her crew, which was hit by *Bismarck* and sunk in 1941.

An initial climb is rewarded with fine views across the Test Valley.

4 Broughton Down

5.25 miles / 8.4km

This walk starts at Broughton Down, a chalk downland Site of Special Scientific Interest. Look out for rare butterflies and plants from May onwards. The walk also passes one of four archaeological remnants of a Bronze Age round barrows lying along the crest of the hill. There are also stunning views across the valley to Broughton and Danebury hillfort. Rising through shady woodland, the walk dips into the downland site, and on into Broughton along tranquil farmland tracks. The walk then follows the Clarendon Way along the Wallop Brook before returning to the village of Broughton with thatched cottages, an historic church and dovecot, and two welcoming pubs.

The Walk

1 From the starting point on **Buckholt Road**, ignore the first farm track to the right. A few metres further up the slope two bridleways fork. Take the right-hand fork, past a Broughton village **millennium sculpture** on the right called *Animal-Vegetable-Mineral*. Continue up the wooded slope lined with yew trees and, after around 400m, look out for a small wooded track on the right,

Broughton Down

The Facts

Terrain A fairly steep but short climb and ascent; paths on the chalk can be slippery in wet weather.

Map OS Explorer 131 Romsey, Andover & Test Valley.

Starting point The roadside parking on Buckholt Road, Broughton (GR SU 302326).

How to get there & parking Broughton is signposted from the A30 to the west of Stockbridge. There is roadside parking for a few cars at Buckholt Road, Broughton. Limited on-street parking at the village green. **Sat nav** SO20 8DA.

Refreshments The Tally Ho ☎ 01794 301280
www.thetallyhobroughton.co.uk
and The Greyhound ☎ 01794 301992
www.greyhoundinnbroughton.co.uk – both in Broughton.

signposted with a yellow footpath marker. Continue along this track uphill as it winds through the trees.

2 At the top of the slope, as the ground starts to slope steeply on the right, enjoy views through a gate on the right, but for the moment continue along the wooded footpath. Pass through a kissing gate in the woodlands, entering the **Wildlife Trust reserve**. At a second wooden kissing gate on the right, pass into the downland area. Turn left along a grassy path which hugs the top of the slope, enjoying the views. Pass through a kissing gate within the reserve, and head for a small mound straight ahead (a Bronze Age round barrow known as the **Plum Pudding**). Pass to the left side of the barrow, and head for the corner of the reserve diagonally to the right.

3 Pass out of the reserve through a kissing gate, and turn right, heading downhill along a wide chalky bridleway towards **Broughton Down Farm**. After the main farm buildings, turn right along a further signposted bridleway, enjoying views back to **Broughton Down**. At a main road turn right, keeping to the wide verges and past the houses on the right. Cross to a pavement and pass a lane on the left-hand side and a cemetery. Just after **Whiteshoot** cul-de-sac turn left down a pathway running between houses. Pass a community orchard area and play park.

4 Turn right along **High Street**, and left down **Rectory Lane** just before the

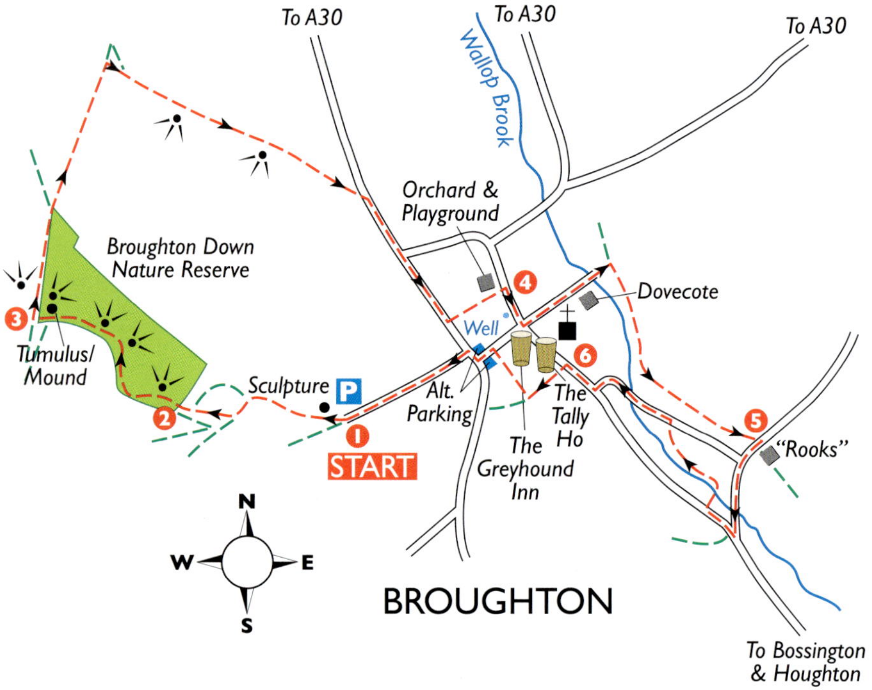

main village crossroads. Pass over a small stream (**Wallop Brook**, a tributary of the River Test), and continue straight on along a footpath between two gated driveways. Turn right along the **Clarendon Way**, and continue straight on with the backs of large houses to the right, and horse fields to the left. Cross a farm track and continue along the field opposite.

5 At a T-junction of paths marked by the **Rooks sculpture**, turn right down a farm track to a meeting of lanes. Continue straight on down **Rookery Lane**, using a footway to cross the **Wallop Brook** at a ford. Turn right onto **Horsebridge Road**, and after 100m or so turn right down a wide driveway to a mill house, back over the brook, and take the footpath to the side of the property, between fences first then opening out. Cross a stile back onto Rookery Lane and turn left. Follow the road round to the left, and turn right onto Horsebridge Road.

6 Continue straight on to the village shop and post office. Turn left onto a footpath to return to the starting point, or continue straight on to find the two village pubs and to explore the church and unusual dovecot. To return to the start, continue along the footpath to open fields, and turn right before a row of red brick houses. Turn left onto **Queenwood Road** to a village green. Turn right onto **Salisbury Road** and left onto Buckholt Road.

What to look out for –

Butterflies

Adonis Blue.

Broughton Down is a Site of Special Scientific Interest for its rare chalk grassland plants and butterflies. The site is noted in particular for its colonies of chalkhill blue and Adonis blue but also rare species such as the silver-spotted skipper, Essex skipper and Duke of Burgundy. Some of these butterflies are only found on chalk grasslands. The chalkhill blue and the Adonis blue, for example, both need horsehoe vetch to feed on, so are limited to the habitats where this plant grows.

Germander Speedwell.

Germander Speedwell

This cheery little flower is associated with roadside verges and used to be known as farewell or goodbye, a flower that would speed you on your way. The bright blue flowers have little white 'bird's eyes' in the middle, and are in flower in May on this chalky hillside alongside wild strawberries, early forget-me-nots and other more specialist flowers associated with chalk.

Views across the South Downs on the route from Beacon Hill to Exton.

5 Beacon Hill

6.25 miles / 10km

Starting at a popular South Downs National Park beauty spot and Site of Special Scientific Interest, Beacon Hill, this invigorating walk has stunning views of Old Winchester Hill and across the downs to the Solent. After a descent into the Meon Valley, the walk passes through the pretty village of Exton with glimpses of the River Meon, past a 13th-century church, and along the former Meon Valley Railway line to Warnford and active watercress beds before a stiff climb back up Beacon Hill. There are two country pubs en route.

The Walk

1 From the car park, turn away from the road and follow the way-marked "**South Downs Way**" track straight ahead through a gate. You will have a woodland to the left-hand side, and open fields visible through trees to the right, gradually opening up to long views across the fields. Continue straight on to the summit of **Beacon Hill**. After admiring the views, continue along the track for a few metres, then turn sharply back on yourself (still following the South Downs Way) and through a gate, to start the descent to **Exton**.

The Facts

Terrain An undulating route involving a steep descent and climb; several stiles to cross and footpaths which can be uneven in places and slippery after rain.

Map OS Explorer OL 32 Winchester and OL 3 Meon Valley.

Starting point Beaconhill Beeches car park (GR SU 598227).

How to get there & parking From the A32 take the B3035 towards Bishop's Waltham. Take the first lane on the right-hand side, Beacon Hill Lane. Turn left then right to find the car park. **Sat nav** SO32 3LJ.

Refreshments The Shoe Inn ☎ 01489 877526 www.theshoeexton.co.uk, and the George and Falcon ☎ 01730 829623 www.georgeandfalcon.com, both en route.

2 On reaching a lane turn left, still going downhill, and after just a few metres look out for signposts on the left for a **'temporary South Downs'** off-road route. Pass through a kissing gate, and continue downhill diagonally across the fields; pass through a kissing gate, double kissing gate, three sets of double stiles, and a further kissing gate to the bottom of the valley. After a slight incline, the path turns left, following a field boundary to the left-hand side to a metal kissing gate and through to Exton village.

The route at point 1.

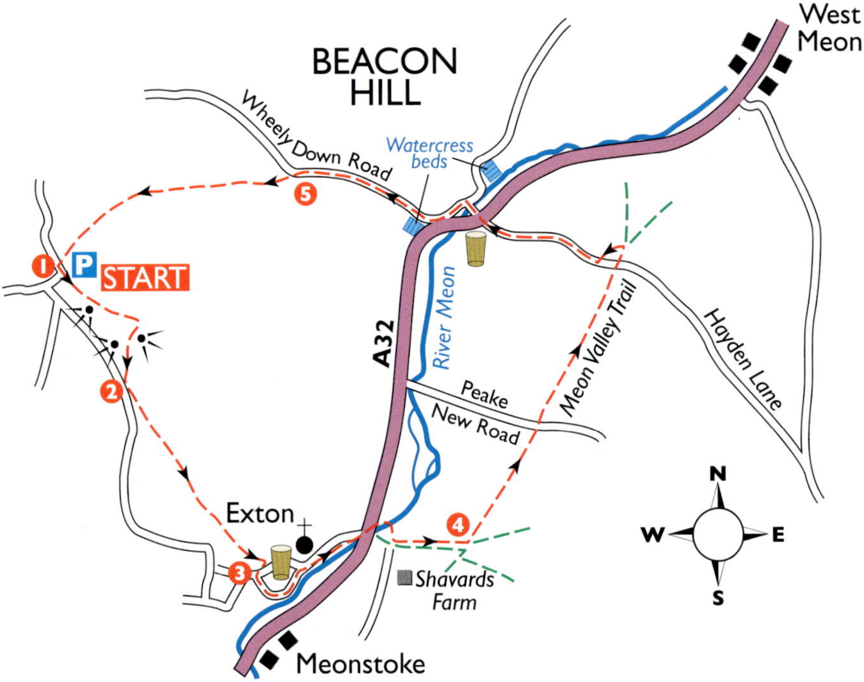

3 Turn right along the lane then left, left and left again through the pretty village of Exton to find the **Shoe** pub then continue on your way. At the next junction of lanes, the **church of St Peter and St Paul** on the left is well worth a visit, or turn right to continue your walk, with occasional glimpses of the **River Meon** on the right. Taking great care on this busy road, cross over the A32 to a well-surfaced pathway directly opposite signed '**No Through Road**'. Follow this footpath for 50m or so, and then turn left signposted 'South Downs Way', before **Shavards Farm**. Continue along this path for a few hundred metres and up a short set of steps to the **Meon Valley Trail**, a former railway line.

4 Turn left and continue along the trail for half a mile. Pass over a lane (**Peake New Road**), and continue for a further half-mile to a high bridge over the trail carrying **Hayden Lane**. Continue for 20m or so beyond the bridge and turn sharp left onto a steep but well-surfaced path signposted '**Warnford**'. On reaching Hayden Lane, turn right and continue straight on to Warnford. Cross over the A32, taking care, and continue straight ahead along the lane before the **George and Falcon** pub into the village centre, and left again to the A32 watching out for watercress beds. Continue along the A32 for a few metres. Turn right along **Wheely Down Road** after **Warnford House**.

5 At **Wheely Down Farm and Forge**, turn left following signs for **Monarch's Way**, passing between the forge and main house and up to the right. Here starts the steep climb back up Beacon Hill. Initially following a farm track, the path diverges off to the right still following the Monarch's Way signposts, and then bends left. Continue up the hill between fields until you reach a wooden gate. Pass into a lovely woodland of hazel, beech and yew. The car park is 50m further on through another wooden gate.

What to look out for –

Watercress beds, Warnford

Watercress is a native plant, thriving in the headwaters of Hampshire's clear chalk streams including the River Meon. It has been an important part of local people's diets for thousands of years. The nearby Meon Valley railway line, built in 1903, provided the ability to transport fresh, perishable goods including watercress to urban markets like London quickly. This led to more commercial growing beds being constructed, such as those seen at Warnford, still in use today.

Looking across to Portsdown Hill on a fine summer's evening.

6 Southwick

5 miles / 8km

The walk starts from the D-Day Memorial Hall, commemorating the events which unfolded on 6 June 1944. The route takes in parts of this pretty village entirely owned by the Southwick Estate, although the house itself was requisitioned in the Second World War and is still in military use. From the village, the walk passes through cool shady woodlands, quiet lanes and gently rolling farmland. The return route has views to Portsdown Hill; particularly visible are the masts of a Royal Navy Type 45 Destroyer, part of the Defence Science and Technology Laboratory. Continuing the naval links, this area was once part of the Norman Royal Hunting Forest of Bere. Timber from these woodlands supplied naval ship-building industries in Portsmouth until metal started to be used in the 19th century – a story told in the nearby Portsmouth Historic Dockyard.

The Facts

Terrain Gently undulating.

Map OS Explorer OL 3 Meon Valley.

Starting point The village car park to the rear of the Golden Lion and Memorial Hall. (GR SU 626085).

How to get there & parking Southwick is just off the B2177, accessed from the A32 at Wickham or from Portsdown Hill to the north of Portsmouth. Park in the village car park (free) to the rear of the Golden Lion and Memorial Hall. Alternatively, there is additional parking in a large lay-by on the B2127. **Sat nav** PO17 6ED.

Refreshments The Golden Lion ☎ 023 9221 0437, and a café at the village store ☎ 023 9237 8866 www.southwickstore.co.uk, both in Southwick.

The Walk

1 With the **D-Day Memorial Hall** on your right, walk through the passageway ahead onto **High Street**. Turn right, and walk past the church and village shop, cross the road and then continue straight on down High Street past the **Red Lion**. Turn right, past **Castle Farm Barn**, and continue along this road for half a mile, passing two housing estates (**Castle Road** and **Boulter Lane**). Look out for a footpath sign on the right, and pass between a copse and the **Southwick Park** estate wall into an arable field.

2 Keeping the estate wall to the right-hand side continue to a footpath sign on the right, leaving the field, and entering into woodland. Follow the well-trodden and well-signposted pathway through **Place Wood** for a further half-mile, ignoring crossing estate paths. The path emerges into an open arable field through a gap in the hedge. Turn left and follow the field boundary as it curves around to the right to a gap in the hedge and a metalled farm track with a solar farm in the field beyond. Turn right, soon passing **Wanstead Farm** and continue to a junction of tracks. Turn left, walking parallel to **Portsdown Hill**.

3 Cross over **Belney Lane**, and through a gap to the side of the metal farm gate opposite. Continue straight on to a ford. Look out for a footpath sign and small footbridge to the right-hand side of the ford. Cross the stream and turn left. Ahead is a junction of two footpaths. Take the right-hand fork,

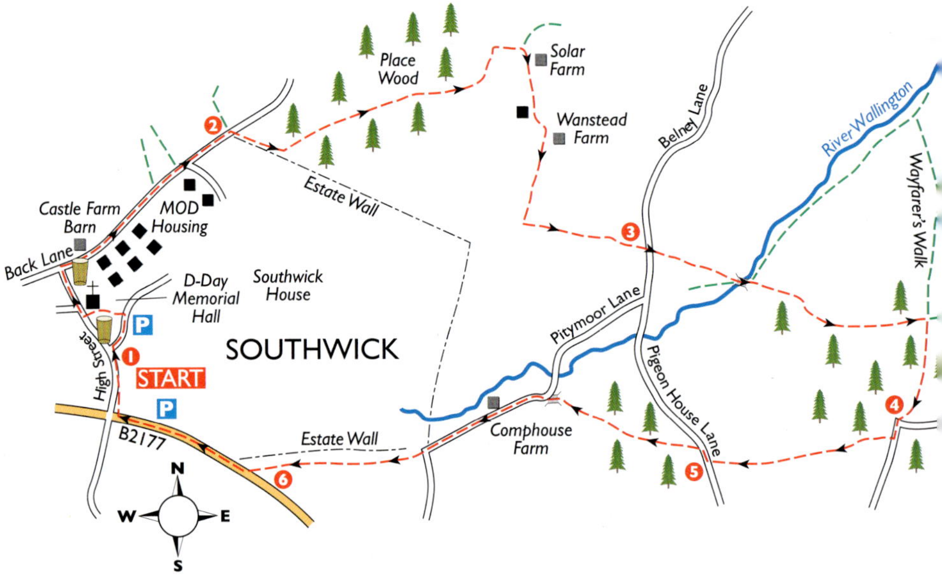

following the edge of the woodland on the right and an open field on the left. Continue straight on for around 200m, then, leaving the field turn right into the woodland. The path curves to the left. Continue to a T-junction with a wide estate ride. Turn left, continuing through the woodland to another T-junction with a vehicle track. Turn right, following the **Wayfarer's Walk** for 300m to a metal gate and **Purbrook Heath Road**.

4 Turn right and immediately look out for footpath signs to the right-hand side. Pass beside another metal gate, moving from woodland into an arable field, and keep to the field edge with the woodland boundary to the right. Pass through a wide hedge boundary into a second field. After 100m, part way across the field. Keep your eyes peeled for a waymarker in the hedge. Pass through into a third field with horses in, and **Hookheath Farm** ahead.

5 At the lane, turn right and, shortly after, turn left, crossing over a stile to a footpath through a third woodland. Continue straight on along this wide pathway for 500m. Look out for a footpath sign to the left and follow the path to a small footbridge over a stream, then turn right to meet **Pitymoor Lane**. Turn left and continue past **Comphouse Farm**. As the lane curves round to the left, pass through a metal farm gate on the right (the formal waymarkers are a few metres further on). Continue straight on, rejoining the Southwick Park estate wall on the right, and an open field on the left.

A mature oak tree lit up by sunshine across a field of barley.

6 As the field narrows, continue straight on, following the wall through a small field copse to the B2177. Turn right, taking care on this road and keeping to the wide verges. Pass a lay-by to the right, and at the roundabout turn right, following the road back into **Southwick village**. Take the first road on the right back to the car park and Memorial Hall.

What to look out for –

The D-Day Memorial Hall

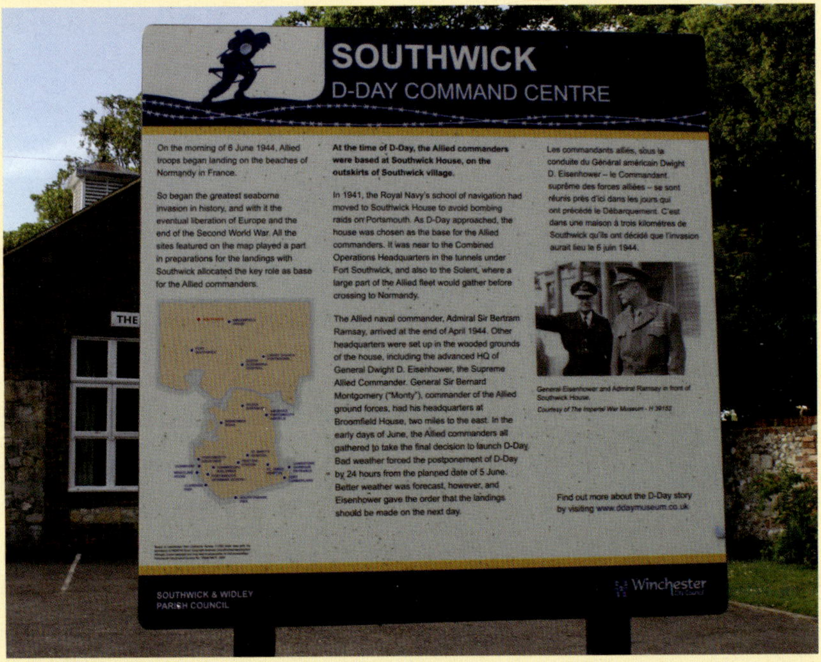

Interpretation panels outside the D-Day Memorial Hall explain the role this area played in that critical military manoeuvre. Southwick was the nerve centre of *Operation Overlord* as military commanders met here to be closer to the ports the troops would leave from along the Hampshire coast. On 6 June 1944, General Dwight D Eisenhower, the Supreme Commander of the Allied Expeditionary Force made his momentous decision to launch the 2,727 ships which turned the tide of the Second World War. Southwick House was the headquarters for the Normandy invasion, with the lounge bar of the Golden Lion becoming the unofficial Officers' Mess.

The pathway takes walkers along the edge of the estuary.

7 River Hamble and Holly Hill Woodland Park

2.75 miles / 4.4km

Starting at Holly Hill Woodland, this family-friendly walk starts by exploring the former Victorian water gardens of Sarisbury Court before heading downhill to the River Hamble Estuary. A stunning pathway takes walkers along the edge of this busy estuary with plenty of boats and wildlife to look at. The walk returns via Wendleholme Nature Reserve and back through the shady woodlands of Holly Hill Woodland Park.

The Walk

1 From the car park, enter the woodland park through the decorative gates, continue straight on along the main path and downhill, ignoring crossing paths

summer

The Facts

Terrain Mainly on well-made paths, but muddy in patches. Moderately undulating, with a long descent to the Hamble and an uphill back to the car park.

Map OS Explorer OL 3 Meon Valley.

Starting point Holly Hill Woodland Park (GR SU 501079).

How to get there & parking The A27 can be accessed from J8 or J9 of the M27; follow the A27 towards Sarisbury then turn down Barnes Lane towards Warsash. The free car park at Holly Hill Woodland Park is signposted from Barnes Lane. **Sat nav** SO31 7BJ.

Refreshments Several picnic tables en route. The Rising Sun in Warsash ☎ 01489 576898 www.oldenglishinns.co.uk, and the Jolly Sailor in Bursledon ☎ 023 8040 5557 www.jollysailoroldbursledon.co.uk, are both nearby with views over the Hamble.

to the left and right for now. On reaching a crossing of paths, turn right downhill following a fence on the left-hand side to a series of landscaped lakes.

Holly Hill Woodland Park was originally part of a large estate linked to Sarisbury Court, and is now owned by Fareham Borough Council and is being restored. The lakes were made from a man-made stone called Pulhamite.

Boats moored in the many marinas lining the estuary.

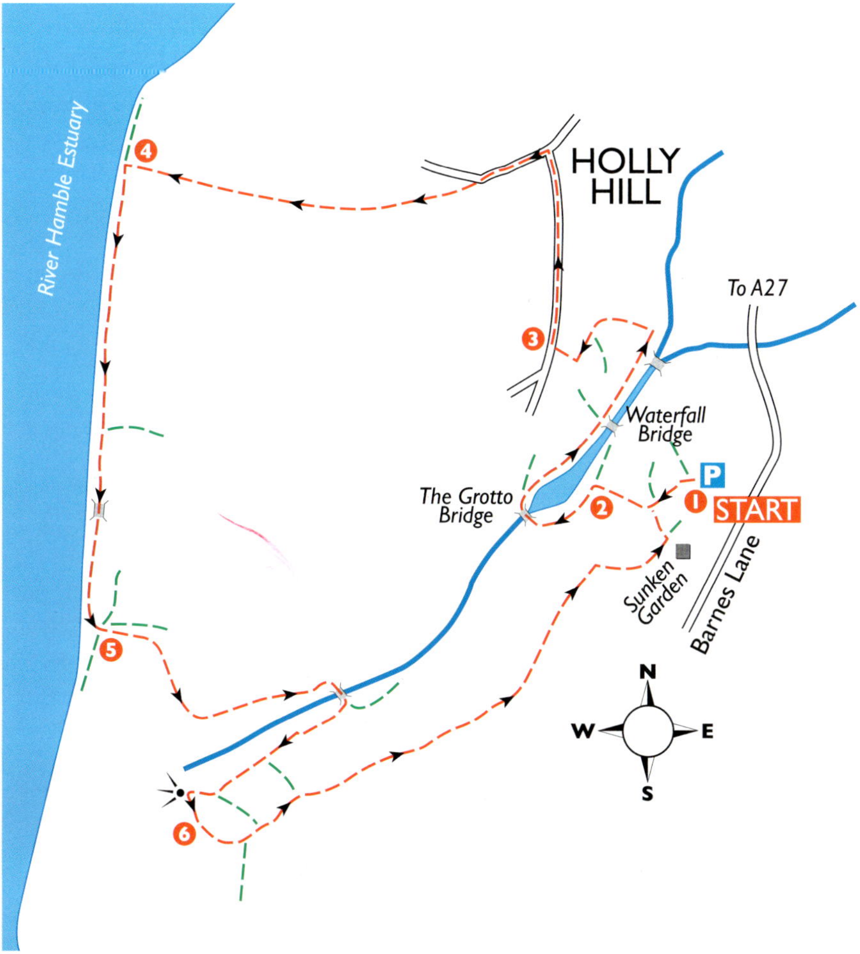

2 Turn initially left, and then right, to a bridge across the southern end of the lakes to **The Grotto**, where guests visiting the gardens would have alighted into rowing boats. Turn right and walk alongside the lake, passing a second bridge and alongside a second lake. At the end of the last lake, turn sharp left, follow the pathway uphill and, at a meeting of paths with two metal barriers, turn right to exit the park via a gate onto **Holly Hill Lane**.

3 Turn right along the road, continue straight on for a few hundred metres, then turn left down **Crableck Lane**, signposted as a byway. When the road forks, continue straight on down the left-hand fork, now becoming a gravel track, and then narrowing again to a pathway between fields.

4 On reaching the **River Hamble**, turn left onto a well-made pathway alongside the estuary edge. Continue for around half a mile in total, enjoying the stunning views across the estuary and marshes, and the bustle of this busy waterway. After a bridge over a side-stream, look out for a public right of way sign on the left, and enter into **Wendleholme Nature Reserve**, managed by Hampshire County Council.

5 Continue straight on past a wooden gate into woodland. Take the right-hand fork of two paths. Continue to follow this path as it winds through a grassy common, back into woodland and then bears left and down into a dip. After walking down a small set of steps, cross a bridge and onto a boardwalk. Here the path starts to go back uphill. At a fork of paths take the right-hand fork and, at the top of the slope, turn right again onto a well-made woodland path. Continue along the path past two pathways to the left to a viewpoint over the **Hamble Estuary**.

6 Continue straight on, now with a fence on your right. At a T-junction of paths, turn left. At a fork in paths, turn right. Keep going straight on up this pathway for half a mile, ignoring joining paths from the left and right, past picnic benches on the left. At a T-junction of paths turn right and, at a second T-junction, turn left. Passing the sunken garden on your right, keep going straight on. A few metres after this, you will come to the path you used to enter the park – turn right to return to the main gates and car park.

What to look out for –

Sea lavender

The lovely mauve flowers of this plant can form large 'drifts' within coastal marshes. It has adapted to be salt-tolerant so is able to live in estuaries like the Hamble. Flowering from July into autumn, it forms clumps, and is related to the thrift family rather than to the lavender plants we know from our gardens. Its Latin name is *Limonium vulgare*. Please respect the environment and don't pick these wild flowers.

Walking through peaceful farmland high up on the downs.

8 Preston Candover

4.25 miles / 6.8km

In July and August, arable crops are ready for harvest, trees are in full leaf, wild flowers are still out, and the quick-of-sight might be rewarded by glimpses of summer farmland birds such as the yellowhammer. This walk takes in peaceful downland countryside starting from the historic rural village of Preston Candover with many interesting listed buildings, two churches and a small village green. The walk rises past a vineyard into picturesque farmland, and rewards with long views over the Candover Valley on the way back to the village. With a country pub awaiting your return, this makes a fine summer walk.

The Walk

1 From the car park, turn left. Walk past a village hall on your left-hand side and turn left through a wooden gate into the recreation ground, heading for the gap in the hedge and bridleway directly opposite. Continue along the bridleway, now climbing uphill beside a vineyard on the right-hand side and a tall hedgerow to the left. At the top of the hill the path bends right then left,

The Facts

Terrain Mainly on well-made paths and farm tracks, but with rough ground and mud in places, and a steady climb.

Map OS Explorer 144 Basingstoke, Alton & Whitchurch.

Starting point Preston Candover village car park (GR SU 607418).

How to get there & parking The B3046 runs through the Candover Valley, from New Alresford to join the A339 just south of Basingstoke. There is a car park in the village of Preston Candover, opposite the school. **Sat nav** RG25 2EE.

Refreshments The Purefoy Arms in Preston Candover ☎ 01256 389777 www.thepurefoyarms.co.uk.

A combine harvester hard at work in a field of wheat.

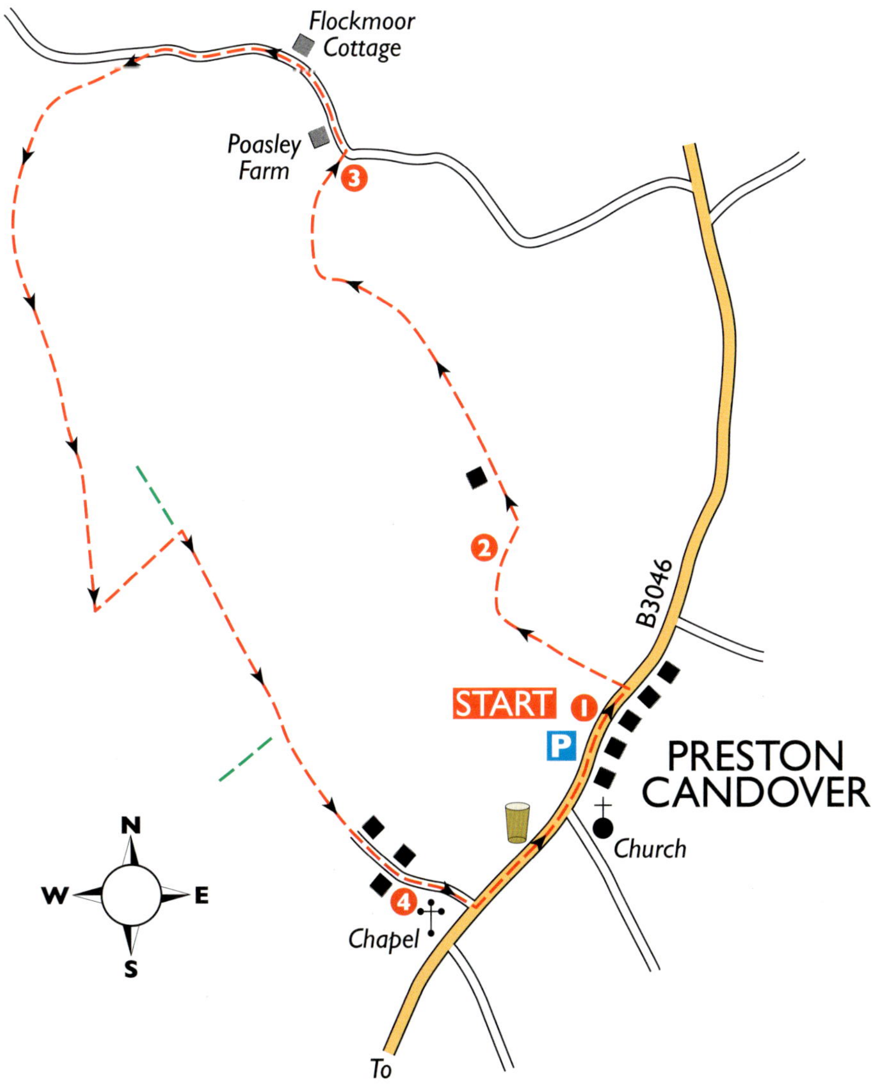

skirting some woodland, to emerge onto concrete tracks near a cluster of large farm buildings.

2 Turn right, then left to skirt the farm buildings and continue straight on along the wide farm access road, keeping the farm buildings to your left-hand side. Continue for around half a mile, passing down into a dip and back up the other side towards a woodland, and enjoying views of open countryside to the

right and left. On reaching the woodland follow the pathway as it loops around the woodland to the right, and then diagonally right down to a rural road just past **Poasley Farm**.

3 Turn left along the road and continue for half a mile, then look out for a byway sign on the left-hand side. Turn left along this byway and, keeping the field boundary close to your right-hand side continue for a mile to a T-junction with a well-made farm track. Turn left and after 200m or so where a footpath crosses the track turn right. Continue along the byway for another mile, enjoying views down the **Candover Valley**, until the byway eventually becomes a surfaced road.

4 Look out for the chancel of the old village church (see box) on your right-hand side, before continuing down the lane. At the end, the lane rejoins the B3046. Turn left through **Preston Candover**, past the 'new' church and pub and continue straight on to your car.

What to look out for –

Historic churches and buildings

The chancel is all that is now left of the old 12th-century church of St Mary the Virgin, which suffered a fire in the 17th century, and was finally replaced by the new church in 1884. The chancel was retained as a mortuary chapel. The inside still contains beautiful medieval floor tiles including a memorial brass to Katherine Dabridgecort (*d.*1607), and fragments of medieval wall paintings. It is now maintained by the Churches Conservation Trust. The more modern church of St Mary the Virgin is also en route at the centre of the village. It is a Grade II* listed building in its own right. Many of the houses in this historic village are also listed, a mixture of thatched cottages and formal halls on a grander scale.

The path onto Ibsley Common from Summerlug Hill.

9 Ibsley and Rockford Commons

4 miles / 6.4km

Heathlands are at their finest in late summer when the heathers are in bloom. This walk in the New Forest National Park visits two commons which rise above the Avon Valley, giving stunning views across the valley and across the heathlands. The walk starts from Rockford, follows the Avon Valley Path and climbs to Ibsley Common to visit the Huff Duff with its WWII connections. Interpretation boards tell intriguing stories of the Huff Duff and its wartime inhabitants. After descending to cross the Dockens Water, the walk returns via Rockford Common.

The Facts

Terrain Some short but steep climbs and descents and some rough ground.

Map OS Explorer OL 22 New Forest.

Starting point Rockford Common National Trust car park (GR SU 164083).

How to get there & parking Take the road signposted 'Linwood and Moyles Court' from the A338 which runs between Ringwood and Fordingbridge. Rockford Common car park will be on your right. **Sat nav** BH24 3NA.

Refreshments The Alice Lisle is 500m from the car park ☎ 01425 474700 www.thealicelisle.co.uk.

The Walk

1 Walk out of the car park back towards the road. Cross the grassy triangle ahead (after admiring the **Moyles Court Oak**, one of the oldest veteran trees of the New Forest) and take the road straight on towards **Mockbeggar** and **Wood Green**, crossing the ford via a footbridge. Pass **Moyles Court School** on the left-hand side and, 100m or so past the school, turn right onto the **Avon Valley Path** via a kissing gate. This leads uphill slightly, between two horse pasture fields. Turn left at the top of the fields and continue to a further kissing gate. Ignore a grassy path up to the right beside the trees and instead take the grassy path ahead through bracken. Continue along this path skirting the side of a hill, with views of horse pasture fields and houses to the left.

2 At a fork in paths at the end of the fields, turn left, keeping the fence to your left-hand side. Pass between a group of majestic oak trees, now heading downhill slightly, and cross the ditch ahead using the wooden path and footbridge, still following signs for the Avon Valley Path. Cross an unmetalled driveway, then continue straight on along the footpath which rises slightly up through bracken and oak. Skirt around the back of the houses, and here we diverge from the Avon Valley Path. Continue straight on in front of a red brick house, **Forest Holm**, to the unmetalled driveway for the house, and continue straight on for 50m. At a junction of tracks, turn right, heading uphill past a low wooden barrier to the open grassy and scrubby plateau of **Summerlug Hill**. This is part of **Ibsley Common**.

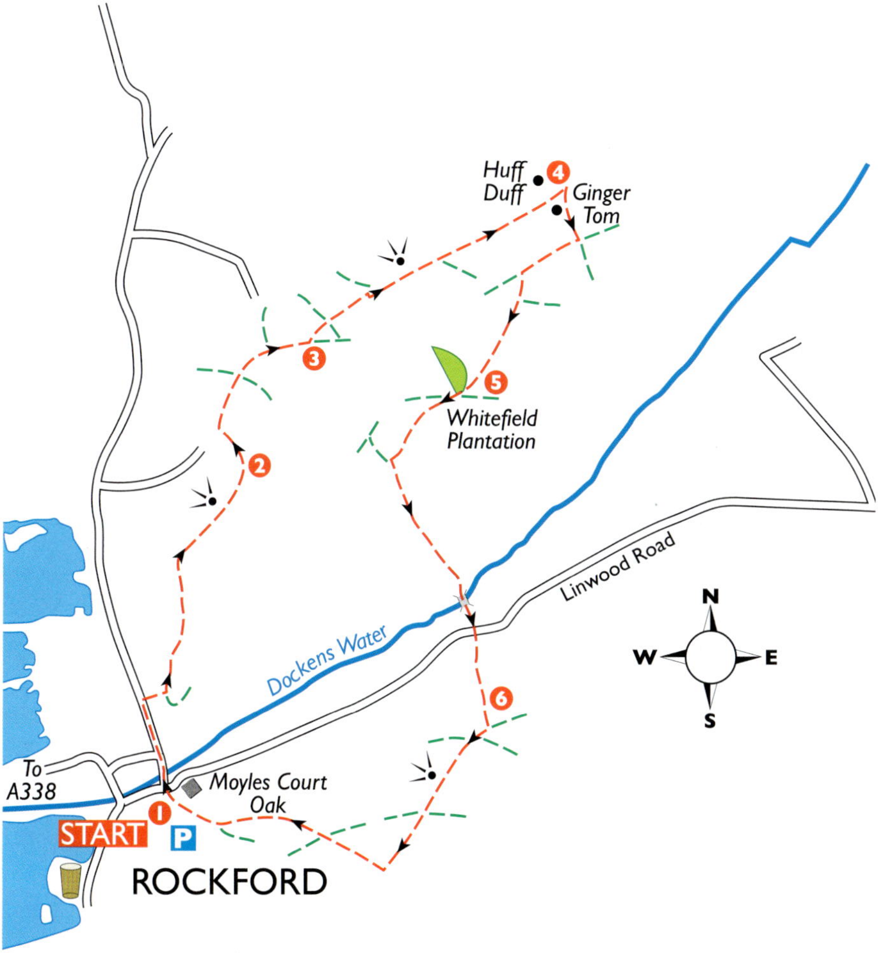

3 Pause here to get your bearings, noting **Whitefield Plantation,** a large clump of trees in the mid-distance. Ignore the path straight on towards the plantation. Take instead the left-hand grassy path, skirting gorse bushes on the right and a small bench, then heading out across the heath in a northeasterly direction, aiming well to the left of the plantation. Follow this path for just over half a mile, passing two slight valleys to the left-hand side, **Little Chibden Bottom** and **Chibden Bottom** and a crossing right of way. Enjoy views to left across the **Avon Valley**.

4 Eventually you will come to an octagonal pillbox-like structure, the **Huff Duff** (see box). Continue straight past, and after a few metres, look out for a

New Forest ponies grazing on Rockford Common.

grassy path sharp to the right-hand side. This soon passes an air-raid shelter on your right, dedicated to **'Ginger Tom'**. At a T-junction of paths turn right, heading now back towards the Whitefield Plantation. Enjoy views over the **Linwood Road** to **Rockford Common** on your left. Around 100m in front of the plantation, take a path diagonally to the left, aiming for the left-hand corner of the plantation.

5 At the plantation corner, continue straight on. There are lots of criss-crossing paths here. We take a well-trodden gravelly path past the start of a valley on the left-hand side. Continue straight on to a further junction of paths. Turn left, now heading southeast back towards Rockford Common, and soon the path heads downhill off the plateau. Cross over **Dockens Water** using the footbridge, then cross the **Linwood Road** and continue straight ahead on a footpath which goes back up the hill on the other side.

6 At the top of the hill, ignore the first path to the right and continue straight on. After a few metres pick up a second path to the right-hand side, a wide gravelly path. The ditch of '**Big Whitemoor Bottom**' lies to the left-hand side,

and you should be soon enjoying views across **Rockford Common** to the right-hand side. Pass beside a wooden barrier as a further path joins from the left, and then look out for a gravel path off to the right-hand side, down into the plateau and across the common. At a patch of scrub and birch trees, the path becomes a clearer vehicle track and descends, bending round to the right and back to the car park. Before you descend to join your car, there are some fantastic views up the hill to the right of the path over the Avon Valley.

What to look out for –

The Huff Duff

During the Second World War, the New Forest was a hive of military activity. The octagonal building is the remnants of the Ibsley High Frequency Direction Finding station (or Huff Duff for short), which in WWII was a three-storey wooden tower. Radio equipment could be used

from here to transmit signals to planes, helping pilots find their way home or locate and intercept enemy aircraft. This Huff Duff was part of a much wider network of similar towers, radar stations and observation posts. The remaining structure is the brick blast wall, to help protect against bomb damage. Nearby is an air-raid shelter for the crew of the Huff Duff telling the story of a ginger tom cat who lived at the Huff Duff and had an ability to hear incoming transmissions before the crew did, helping to save lives. The nearby RAF Ibsley airfield was located around what is now Blashford Lakes as it was subsequently earmarked for gravel extraction. Moyles Court School was the headquarters.

The walk passes through peaceful farmland on the way to Hazeley Bottom.

10 Hartley Wintney and Hazeley Heath

4.5 miles / 7.2km

This walk starts in the pretty village of Hartley Wintney, skirts through the wooded edges of Hazeley Heath to peaceful rural farmland, and returns through the centre of Hazeley Heath, one of north Hampshire's largest heathland remnants. Parts of the site are managed as an RSPB nature reserve, so do bring your binoculars for sightings of rare birds. In late summer, the heather's purple blooms are still vivid, mixed with yellow gorse flowers coming into bloom. Hazeley Heath also has a wartime history and there are remnants of this along the way.

The Facts

Terrain Farmland and unmade paths, can be muddy especially in the healthland areas. Undulating with gentle ascents and descents. A number of stiles.

Map OS Explorer Map 144 Basingstoke.

Starting point Hartley Wintney car park (GR SU 767570).

How to get there & parking Hartley Wintney is on the A30, 10 minutes drive from Junction 4a or 5 from the M3. There is a pay and display car park on Monachus Lane, which is signposted directly from the village centre. **Sat nav** RG27 8NN.

Refreshments The Waggon and Horses in Hartley Wintney at the start or finish ☎ 01252 842119, plus a range of cafés.

The Walk

1 Start by walking north from the car park away from the village centre, up **Chapter Terrace**, heading uphill slightly. Turn right onto **Hartford Road**, and immediately left onto **Primrose Drive**. Turn right onto **Springfield Avenue**, and left up a concrete driveway just before a bend in the road, leading to a children's play area. Pass behind the play area and continue uphill on a narrow pathway leading into birch woodlands. On reaching a T-junction with a wider footpath, turn left, and immediately left again along a wooded gravelled footpath, signposted as a public right of way. Continue straight on, following a line of large mature trees and holly bushes on the left-hand side. On reaching a cluster of dwellings, continue straight on between two sculpted posts. The path becomes a wider vehicle driveway for the houses at this point.

2 Cross over the **B3011**, taking care. Turn right along the pavement, and after a few metres look out for a footpath sign on the left, leading into a heathy common. Take the left-hand fork of two grassy paths to a quiet road. Cross to a white cottage directly opposite, and turn left along a farm track. Look out for a footpath sign in the hedge on the right and pass into a horse-pasture field. Keeping the field boundary close to your right, continue straight on downhill to the bottom of the field. Cross a stile and turn right then pass into a second field. Turn left, skirting the field boundary, and continue to the far end of the field, past a single house on the right. Pass through the hedge via a small footbridge into a meadow and continue straight on. Pass through a kissing gate on the right-hand side.

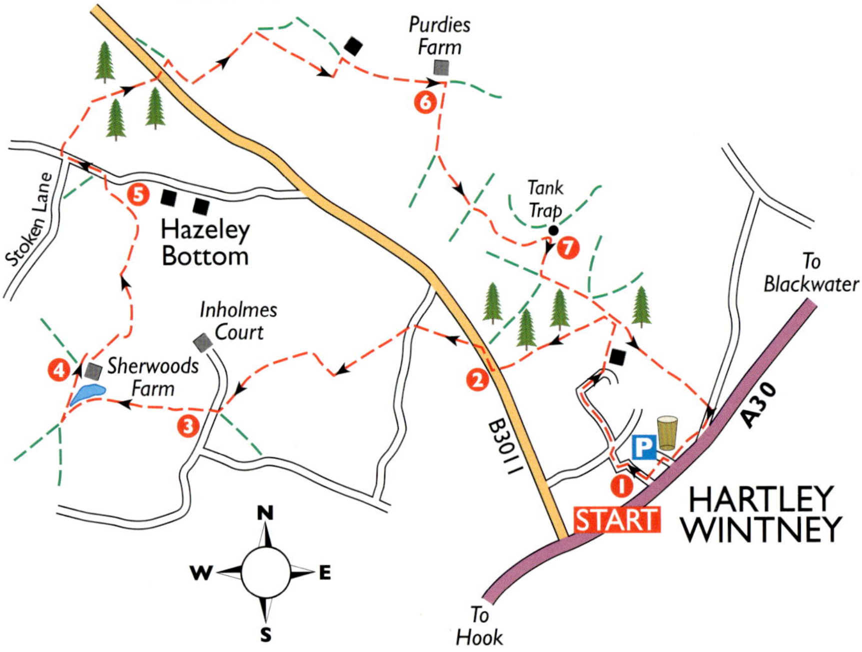

3 Turn left along the driveway to **Inholmes Court** and immediately right through a kissing gate in the hedge into an arable field. Keep the field boundary close on your right-hand side, and continue straight on. At the end of the field, pass through a gap in the hedge on the right, cross a ditch via a small footbridge and turn left passing a lake and views of **Sherwoods Farm**. On reaching a driveway, turn right and walk towards the farm, passing to the left of the farm.

4 Just before the outbuildings, turn through a gap in the hedge on your left. Turn right in the field, right again, keeping to the field edge, and continue straight on towards the hamlet of **Hazeley Bottom**. Three quarters of the way down the field, cross a stile on your right, then pass through double gates and turn left. Keep the ditch and hedge close on the left-hand side. Cross a stile and after 25m or so, turn right across the field, crossing a ditch and a further stile. Continue straight on between fields. The path then skirts the gardens of Hazeley Bottom, turning left then right and leading to a small set of steps down onto a rural road.

5 Turn left away from the hamlet. Opposite **Stoken Lane**, turn right onto a footpath between fields. After 200m or so, turn right away from the sunken lane up a slight incline into woodland. Follow this path to a driveway and turn left along it. Take care at the B3011, crossing to a narrow footpath directly opposite

A beech-lined track on the edge of Hazeley Heath.

into woodland. After a few metres, on reaching a T-junction of paths at the edge of the heathland, turn right and continue for around 70m to a distinct crossing of paths in a slight dip in the landscape. Turn left here, crossing the heath. At a further T-junction of paths, turn right, and continue straight along this pathway to a driveway. Turn left here, then right along a wooded footpath, skirting the edge of the property. Continue straight on to **Purdies Farm**.

6 Turn right along the wooded driveway back across the heath. After 250m or so, turn left past two bollards and follow the grassy footpath into the heathland. At a fork in the grassy paths, take the right-hand fork. Cross over an intersecting grassy path and continue straight on. At a second intersection of paths, continue straight on. At a further fork of paths, turn left, emerging at a concrete pathway and the remnants of a tank trap.

The ramp was used for tank evaluation and testing the breaking strains of steel cables during WWI and II. Troops were also trained in tank rescue from boggy ground on the heath.

7 Turn right along the concrete path and left along a wide gravelled path. Pass a footpath sign on the left, and a bridleway sign on the left. Continue into woodland. The path turns slightly to the left with a large wooded field bank on the right-hand side. Follow the pathway downhill to a kissing gate, then pass between houses and a play area. Turn right along **Hare's Lane** back into **Hartley Wintney** and turn right along **Monachus Lane** or between shops further up the high street to the car park.

What to look out for –

Nightjar

These curious and elusive birds are rarely seen in the daytime, but at dusk in the summer months they make an eerie 'churring' sound, and mating pairs make a wing-clapping sound. They are sometimes seen swooping to catch moths to eat. The nightjar is a migrant to the UK from Africa, arriving in the UK from April to breed. They are ground-nesting birds, living in lowland heath and young forestry habitats, and particularly like areas with some taller prominent trees to make their churring calls from. Please keep dogs on the lead or under close control on the main pathways in the heathland so as not to disturb these rare and special birds.

Views from Hurdle Way across to Twyford Down and St Catherine's Hill.

autumn

11 Compton

5 miles / 8km

From September onwards, tree leaves slowly start to change colour, making up for the loss of summer with glorious displays, and this walk is particularly beautiful in autumn. It also passes several of Compton's ancient evergreen yews on the way up to Yew Hill on Compton Down, with stunning views over Winchester landmarks such as St Catherine's Hill, Twyford Down and the St Cross Hospital. The return route is along an avenue of fine beech trees at their most colourful in autumn, along quiet wooded paths and a chance to see more of this parish's beautiful ancient yews.

The Walk

1 Starting from the back of a small information centre within the park and ride, take the footpath directly ahead out of the car park up to **Otterbourne Road**, watching out for buses at the top. Turn left along the pavement. Opposite the driveway for **Compton House** and **Otterbourne House** cross the road, taking care, to a concrete driveway with a metal gate and a stile to the right-

The Facts

Terrain Some short but steep climbs and long, gentle descents. Can be muddy in places.

Map OS Explorer OL 32 Winchester.

Starting point South Winchester Park and Ride (GR SU 472260).

How to get there & parking There is a park and ride car park which is signposted from Junction 11 of the M3, just off the A3090 to Romsey. Very limited on-street parking on Compton Street. **Sat nav** SO21 2FG.

Refreshments None on the route but the Bugle Inn in Twyford is only a five-minute drive away ☎ 01962 714888 www.bugleinntwyford.co.uk.

hand side. As the driveway bends to the left, continue straight on through a metal gate. Turn left through a field and pass through a gate, kissing gate and over a stile to **Compton Street**, opposite the school. Turn right, and then cross the road into the grounds of **All Saints Church**.

2 Facing the front door of the church turn right, through a gate into **Carmans Lane**, noting a number of fine historic buildings, and turn left. The lane soon

Ancient yew trees line many of the pathways in the parish of Compton.

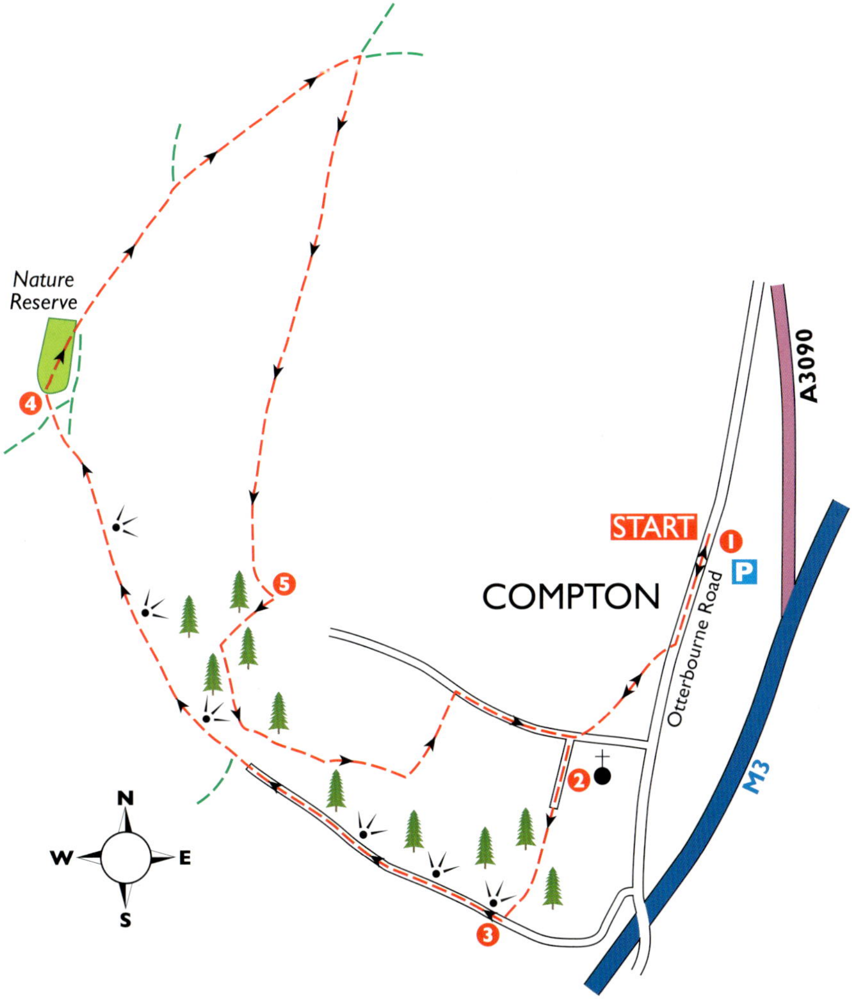

turns from a driveway into a sunken wooded pathway between fields. At a fork in the paths, note the first of the ancient yew trees on the right-hand side, then continue straight on up steep steps ahead. Pass through a kissing gate into a field, and continue the climb to a bench. After enjoying the views, pass through a further kissing gate onto **Hurdle Way**.

3 Turn right along Hurdle Way and continue for just under half a mile past the houses on the left-hand side. The lane turns into a bridleway. Continue straight on again for a further half-mile past a wooden gate and looking out for large yew trees in the hedge-bank to the left. At a fork in paths, continue straight on to a further junction of paths. Take the first pathway to the right into a small butterfly reserve, **Yew Hill**.

4 Continue along the main track of the reserve downhill to a stile, and straight on through a narrow path through scrub to emerge into an open field. Continue straight on down the hill towards the houses of **Oliver's Battery** in the mid-distance, soon rejoining the main bridleway. Continue straight on for 300m or so to a fork in paths. Take the right-hand fork and continue to a further junction of a bridleway and a restricted byway. Turn sharp right down the beech-lined byway with further views across the downs on the left-hand side. Continue for around a mile.

5 Take a path on the right-hand side down a 'tunnel' of trees back into woodland, and turn left. A steep climb is rewarded by more yew trees on the left-hand side. At a fork turn left, with the path still bounded by yews on the left. At a further fork, turn left, downhill. Ignore the first path off to the left and continue straight on, along a wooded pathway leading between fields. Follow the path round to the left to **Compton Street**. Turn right to the church and retrace your steps back to the park and ride.

What to look out for –

Ancient yews

Taxus baccata, is an evergreen conifer tree native to the UK. Yew trees have long been associated with churchyards, but in Compton they border paths which have been used for centuries as cart tracks and drove roads. Some individual trees are thought to be between 500 and 800 years of age. Most parts of the yew tree are poisonous, especially the small seed inside the red aril or seed case (shown above) so best to look but not touch. Yew trees thrive on chalk, so are common across Hampshire. Yew trees are unusual in having male and female trees.

Mature beech trees on the Hinton Ampner estate.

12 Hinton Ampner and Kilmeston

4.5 miles / 7.2km

October and November are great months to see autumn colours on the Hinton Ampner estate in the South Downs National Park. This walk starts at Hinton Ampner house and gardens, passing through open fields, and farmland with views over the rolling hills of the South Downs. Quiet lanes lead to historic Kilmeston village and grand views of Hinton Ampner House await your return. The route takes you through the designed estate landscape with its carefully planted clusters of trees. You could also make a day of it with a visit to this National Trust-owned house, gardens and café.

The Walk

1 From the car park, find a grass path on the left-hand side leading away from **Hinton Ampner**, across the estate to a stile. Cross into a lane, **Hinton Hill**,

autumn

The Facts

Terrain Gently undulating, mainly on well-surfaced paths and lanes, with no steep climbs or ascents and occasional stiles.

Map OS Explorer OL 32 Winchester.

Starting point National Trust car park at Hinton Ampner (GR SU 595276).

How to get there & parking Hinton Ampner is signposted from the A272 near Cheriton between Winchester and Petersfield. Park at the National Trust car park. Check the National Trust website for their charging policy. **Sat nav** SO24 0LA.

Refreshments The Hinton Arms, close by on the A272 ☎ 01962 771252 www.hintonarms.co.uk. The café at Hinton Ampner House (National Trust members/paid entrance) ☎ 01962 771305.

opposite the elegant 18th-century **Hinton Ampner Place**. Turn right, walking uphill, and follow the lane round to the left past a large veteran oak tree. After a few metres, as the lane bends to the right, continue straight on past **Godwin's Farm** on the left (a listed 17th-century farmhouse) to a bridleway. You will have a hedgerow on the left and views across open fields to the right. Continue straight on along the ridge of the hill. At the end of the first long field, ignore

Sheep posing for the camera in the grounds of the Hinton Ampner estate.

Hinton Ampner and Kilmeston

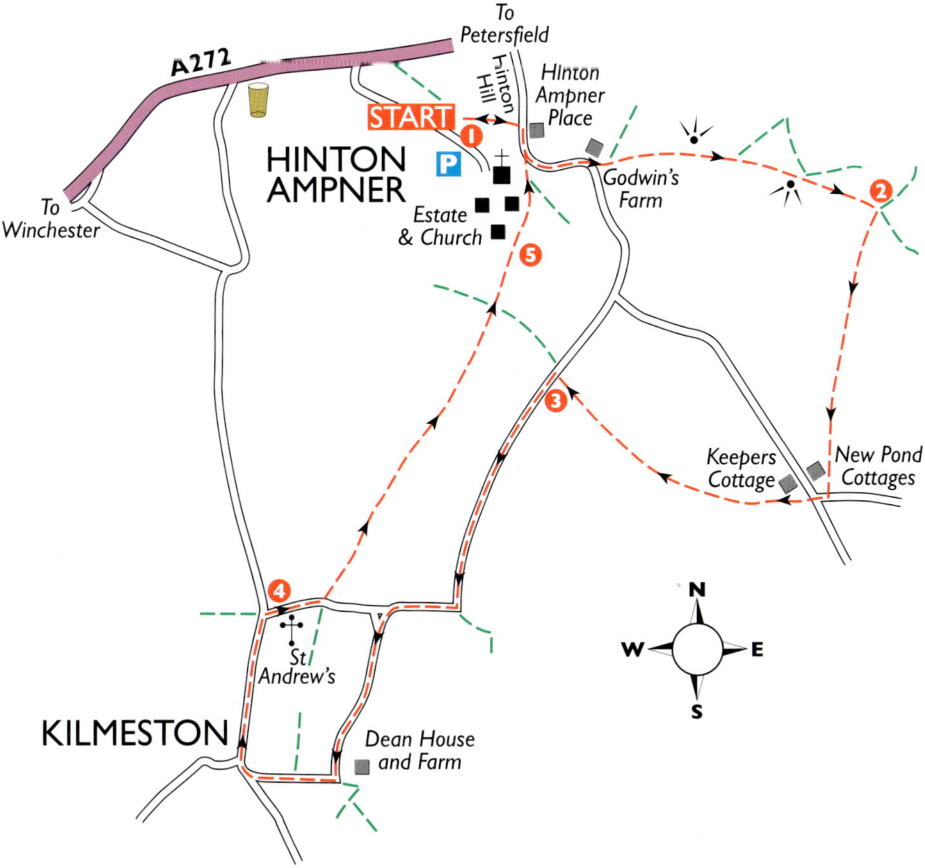

crossing paths and continue straight on into a second long field, keeping the field boundary to the left-hand side.

2 At the end of the second field, turn right, down into a dip of the valley, over a gentle rise and downhill, keeping the field boundary on your right-hand side. On reaching a lane, turn right, past **New Pond Cottages**. As the lane turns to the right continue straight on along a restricted byway to the back of **Keepers Cottage**. Continue straight on for a third of a mile past fields and woodlands to a lane.

3 Turn left, now moving uphill, with beech trees on either side. After half a mile, the lane bends to the right and we follow. At a fork turn left, and continue to **Dean House and Farm**. Turn right here and, at a further junction of lanes, right again, taking in a loop of the village. Pass the village hall on the right-hand side and village green. Turn right again to find **St Andrew's Church**.

4 A few metres after the church, look out for a footpath to the left signposted '**Wayfarers Walk**'. Cross the stile into open fields and continue straight on to a further stile, with views to **Hinton Ampner House** in the mid-distance. Cross the next field diagonally to the right of the house, aiming for a clump of trees. Pass through the copse to a kissing gate, and keep going diagonally across the next field, still aiming to the right of the house, the path now clearly marked by posts.

5 Pass through a kissing gate and gate and follow the path, with **Hinton Ampner gardens** now to the left. At the top of the rise, pause to admire the **Church of All Saints** to the left-hand side, and then continue downhill to the stile opposite **Hinton Ampner Place**, and cross back over and retrace your steps to the car.

What to look out for –

Historic buildings

Both Hinton Ampner and Kilmeston are historic villages, with many buildings on this route listed for their special interest, from the grand Hinton Ampner House and Kilmeston Manor to 17th-century labourers' cottages. Hinton Ampner House is a grand Georgian-style country house. The property once belonged to a Parliamentarian leader, Sir William Waller, before the Battle of Cheriton in March 1644. The current house was rebuilt in the 18th, 19th and 20th centuries, and is known for its fine gardens and estate. The Church of All Saints is of Saxon origin, whilst St Andrew's church is much later, dating from the 18th century.

Autumnal colours in the Blackwater Arboretum.

13 Rhinefield

2 miles / 3.2km

This family-friendly walk is all about seeing the autumn colours of the New Forest at their finest. It takes in the stunning trees of Blackwater Arboretum, continues with a short stroll through two wooded "inclosures" and returns via a part of the majestic Tall Trees Trail, which boasts some of the tallest trees in the UK. With trees starting to change their colours from mid-September onwards, a mid-October visit will see this walk at its most colourful.

The Walk

1 From the centre of the car park, pick up the signs for the **Blackwater Arboretum**. With your back to the pay and display unit cross the road and continue straight on along the wide avenue to the arboretum. Pass through the gate and take your time here to explore the circular trail at your leisure.

The Facts

Terrain Flat, and on good well-made paths most of the way round. One short stretch can be muddy after rain.

Map OS Explorer OL 22 New Forest.

Starting point Forestry Commission Blackwater car park. (GR SU 268047).

How to get there & parking From Lyndhurst take the A35 towards Christchurch, and after two miles turn left into the Rhinefield Ornamental Drive (signposted 'Rhinefield and Rhinefield House Hotel'). The Blackwater car park is located on the left-hand side, approximately half a mile along Rhinefield Drive. Pay by donation policy. Can get busy at peak times. **Sat nav** SO42 7QB. Alternative car park at Brock Hill, joining the walk at point 3.

Refreshments Coffee and ice-cream vans in the car park (at peak times only). Nearby pubs include the Oak Inn at Bank ☎ 023 8028 2350 www.oakinnlyndhurst.co.uk, the Swan Inn at Emery Down ☎ 023 8028 2203 www.theswanlyndhurst.co.uk, and a range of pubs, restaurants and cafés in Lyndhurst.

Walking through the Vinney Ridge Inclosure.

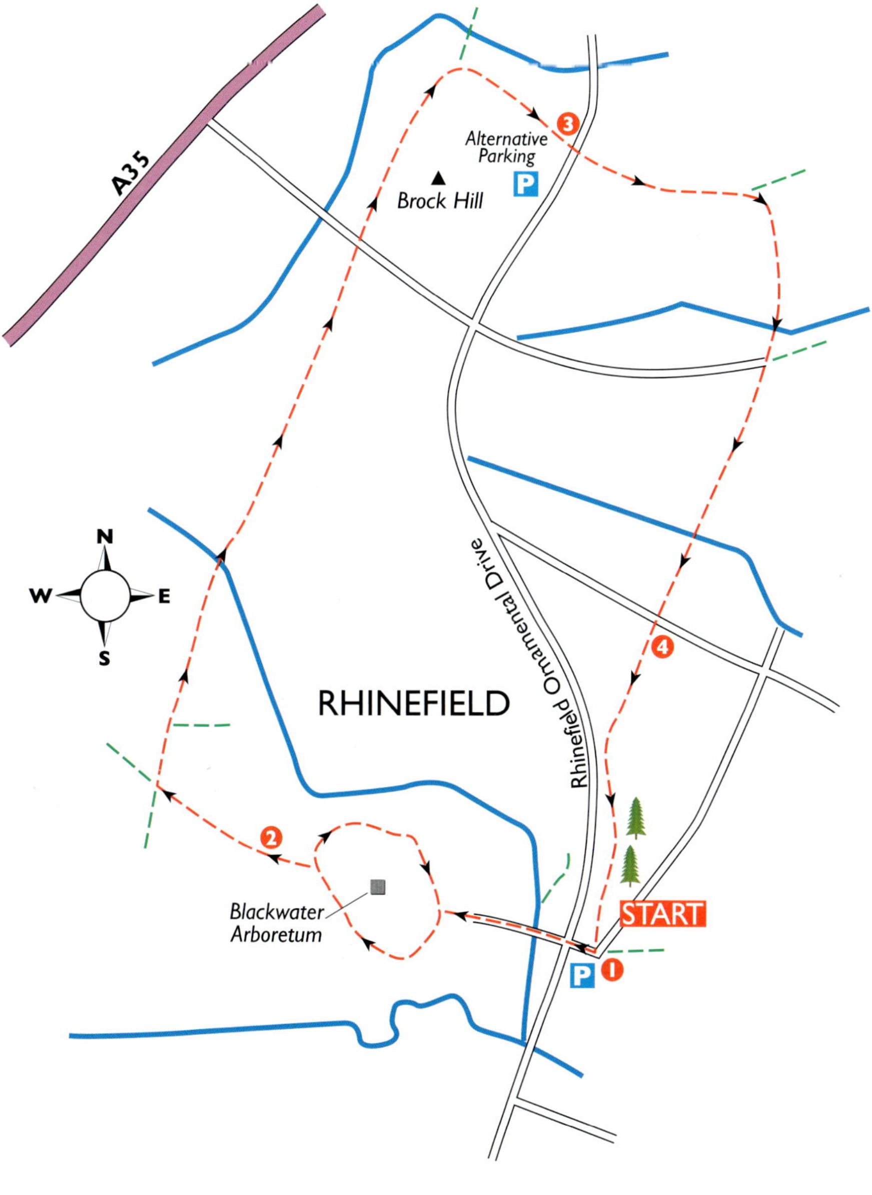

2 Exit the gate on the other side of the arboretum and continue straight on along a wide surfaced path. At a T-junction of paths turn right. ***You will be sharing the pathway with cyclists so do keep an eye out from time to time.*** Continue straight on along this pathway past a wide grassy path to the right-hand side, and two crossing forest rides, and as the path bends to the right, follow it round. After 200m, the path is crossed by the **Rhinefield Ornamental Drive** with **Brock Hill** car park on the right.

3 Cross the road, and continue straight on, still on the wide surfaced path. After 250m or so, the path bends again to the right; follow it round, and continue straight on, past a wide ride crossing the path. After a further 350m, the cycle path turns to the left.

4 Leaving the wide path at this point, continue straight on along the wide grassy ride straight ahead to a T-junction of paths. Turn left, with the Rhinefield Ornamental Drive visible to the right-hand side. Continue straight on back to the car park. *This section of the path follows the Tall Trees Trail.*

What to look out for –

The tallest Douglas fir trees in England

Douglas fir is an evergreen conifer species native to western North America. It has very thick, corky bark, which protects it from fire and insect damage. The species is valuable for timber and the wood is hard and durable. The specimens here are thought to be the tallest in England at 60m.

A field of sheep on the lower slopes of Warner's Hanger.

14 East Worldham

4 miles / 6.4km

Starting from the historic village of East Worldham, with connections to the Chaucer family, this walk explores quiet, wooded countryside in the South Downs National Park. After exploring an historic 13th-century church, the walk enjoys views of a local landmark, an Iron Age hillfort known as King John's Hill, follows a section of the Hangers Way through mature woodlands and returns via some of the steep-sided slopes covered by ancient woodland. These are locally known as 'hangers'. A peaceful walk through rural countryside and another good place to enjoy the colours of autumn.

The Walk

1 Starting from the front of the pub, cross over **Blanket Street** and, after 100m,

The Facts

Terrain Undulating terrain on rural rights of way with some short but steep climbs. Can be muddy in places.

Map OS Explorer OL 33 Haslemere and Petersfield.

Starting point The Three Horseshoes, East Worldham (GR SU 748381).

How to get there & parking East Worldham lies on the B3004 between Alton and Kingsley. The Three Horseshoes is directly on the B3004 two miles east of Alton. Please ask before parking. Limited alternative parking in the village (roadside at Wyck Lane). **Sat nav** GU34 3AE.

Refreshments The Three Horseshoes ☎ 01420 83211. www.threehorseshoesalton.co.uk.

cross the B3004 with care and turn left down **Wyck Lane**. Passing a beautiful old oasthouse on the left-hand side, continue past two housing estates. Turn right down a driveway signposted **Hangers Way** with a large wooded signboard for a number of properties. Turn left from the driveway onto a footpath and skirt the side of the property. At a crossroads of paths, turn right through a kissing gate to explore the beautiful **St Mary's Church**, and then return to the path. Continue down the hill, through a gate, down wooden steps to a kissing gate and continue to emerge at **The Old School House**.

2 Cross the road, taking care, and turn right. After a few metres, turn left along the upper of two driveways, signposted Hangers Way. Pass through a kissing gate on the left and continue across the field following a fence-line, aiming to the right of **King John's Hill**. In the left-hand corner of the field, pass through another kissing gate and continue past the lake. Pass through a metal gate and follow the path round to the right of the hill, along a line of oaks. Pass through a kissing gate, and follow the path round to the left into woodland. After 50m, turn right down the first wide ride, downhill to a kissing gate. Continue straight on across the field to a double gate, and straight on across the next field to a kissing gate and footbridge across a low ditch.

3 Follow the Hangers Way signposts throughout this section. Continue straight on into scrubby woodland (ignoring the path diagonally to the left) following a grassy path through into mature open woodland. Views open out into a wide grassy field surrounded by trees. Turn off to the right, through a kissing gate into woodland. After a few metres, turn to the left, and then turn

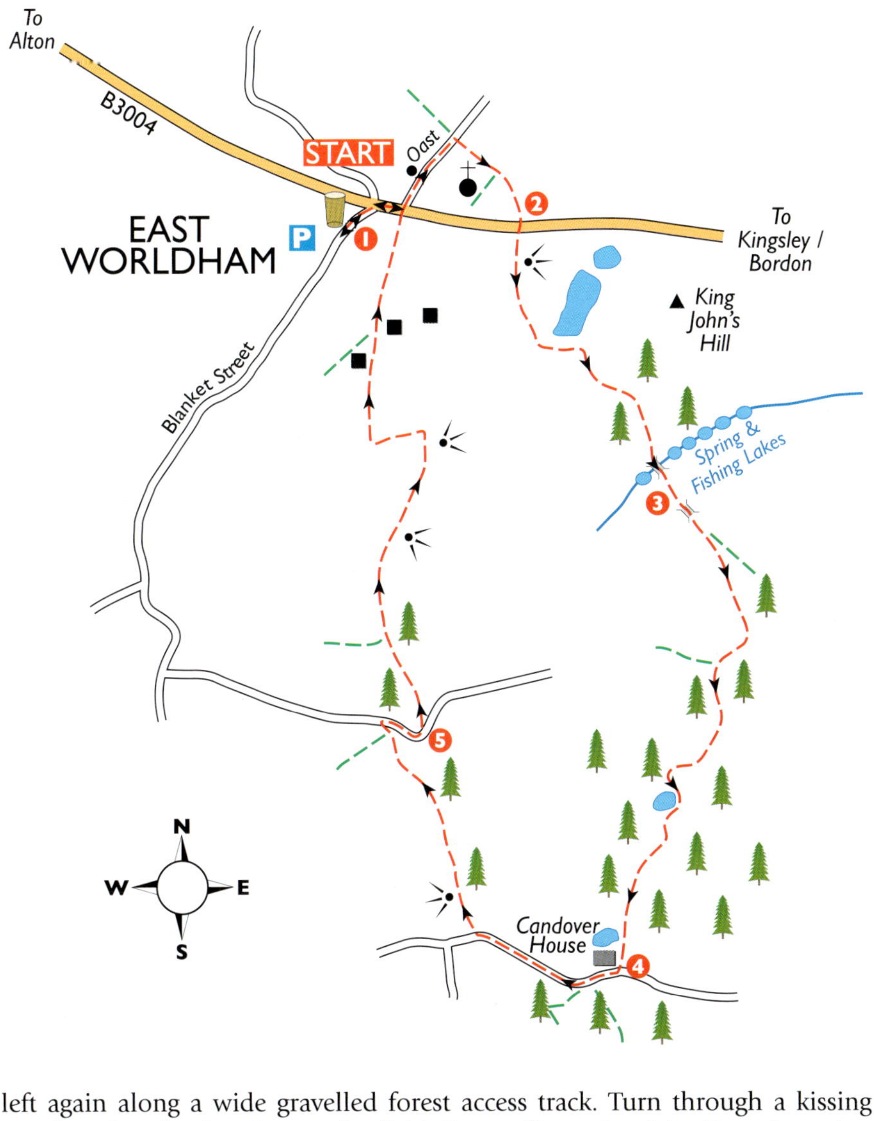

left again along a wide gravelled forest access track. Turn through a kissing gate into farmland and cross the field diagonally to the right. Pass through a kissing gate onto a wide gravelly ride. Halfway up the ride, turn left into the woodland, now following a narrower winding footpath. Pass a fishing lake before emerging back onto a wide ride. Continue to follow the Hangers Way signs as the path turns left, right and left again along a wide grassy ride. Passing a pond on the right and views to **Candover House**, go through a gate and onto a rural lane.

Following the Hangers Way through quiet woodland and farmland.

4 Now leaving the Hangers Way, turn right along the lane for 400m. As the lane gets steeper with high banks, look out for a footpath running up the side of the right-hand bank Park Hanger. At the top, turn right along a large field with open vistas to the left. Continue straight on, and at the end of the field, as the path curves to the left, turn right, keeping to the field boundary, and cut through a gap in the hedge to a narrow lane.

5 Turn right along the lane with a steep descent. As the lane bends left, turn left down a farm track and footpath just above the lane. Cross a stile into a pasture field. Keeping to the field boundary on the left-hand side, cross a second stile on the left into woodlands and climb the steep path back up Warner's Hanger. Turn right at the top of the hill. Continue straight on into the next field, and follow the path as it bends sharply to the left, still with the field boundary on your right. Turn right at the end of the field, walking towards the houses. Cross a farm track to a footpath between a fence and hedge. Cross three stiles and descend steep steps back onto the B3004. Turn left to return to the pub.

What to look out for –

The Mysterious Lady

Within the church of St Mary the Virgin, there lies an effigy of a mysterious medieval lady. Once thought to be that of Philippa Roet, wife of the famous 14th-century poet Geoffery Chaucer, the date and style of clothing is now thought to be too early. Thomas Chaucer, son of Geoffrey and Philippa, did inherit the manor of East Worldham through marriage. Thomas Chaucer was Speaker of the House of Commons and Chief Butler of England for almost 30 years, serving Richard II and Henry IV.

The Royal Victoria Country Park at point 1 on the walk.

15 Netley Abbey and Royal Victoria Country Park

2 or 4.5 miles / 3.2 or 7.2km

A **semi-urban walk linking** parks and paths around Netley, taking in Netley Abbey – a ruined medieval monastery, views over busy Southampton Water, The Hard at Netley, and Royal Victoria Country Park, with its past military connections. The park was once home to the Royal Victoria Hospital. With several woodland stretches, this walk is particularly enjoyable in autumn, perhaps even around Remembrance Day in November, as the walk passes Netley Military Cemetery connected to the hospital, a poignant reminder of the losses experienced during the First and Second World Wars.

Netley Abbey and Royal Victoria Country Park 15

autumn

The Facts

Terrain Gently undulating, no steep climbs or ascents. Muddy in places. Contains a very short stretch on a B road with no pavement.

Map OS Explorer OL 22 New Forest.

Starting point Royal Victoria Country Park car park (GR SU461077).

How to get there & parking Netley is between Southampton and Hamble-Le-Rice on Hampshire's coastline. Signposted from Junction 8 of the M27, or from the A27. There is parking at Royal Victoria Country Park pay and display car park. There are also two train stations directly on the route at Hamble and Netley with regular trains to Southampton and Portsmouth. **Sat nav** SO31 5GA.

Refreshments Royal Victoria Country Park Café ☎ 023 8045 4296 or The Prince Consort, Netley ☎ 023 8045 2676 www.theprinceconsortpub.co.uk.

The Walk

1 From the car park, turn left away from the access road, enjoying views over **Southampton Water** to the right. Turn left towards the hospital chapel, walking uphill slightly. Turn right before the chapel, walking towards woodland, and turn left at the end of the path. Pass a large wooden gate to a junction of paths and take the right-hand tarmac path past another large gate, signposted to the military cemetery. Continue along this path, uphill slightly and raised up from mature woodland on the right and left. Ignore a tarmac cycle route off to the right and continue towards a set of bright green ornamental gates leading into the cemetery.

2 Keep to the left-hand path and, at the end of the cemetery, pass through a small green gate onto a woodland path. Take the left-hand fork, downhill, and turn right onto a boardwalk. Follow this path as it meanders through the woodland, crossing three small footbridges over streams and ditches. Cross over a tarmac access road to a footpath opposite, and follow this as it bends to the left, over a large footbridge to join the **Hamble Rail Trail**.

3 **Hamble train station** is 50m to the right along this path. Turn left and continue straight on along this wooded path with the railway line to your right-hand side. The path passes a police training centre on the left. Just after a sports

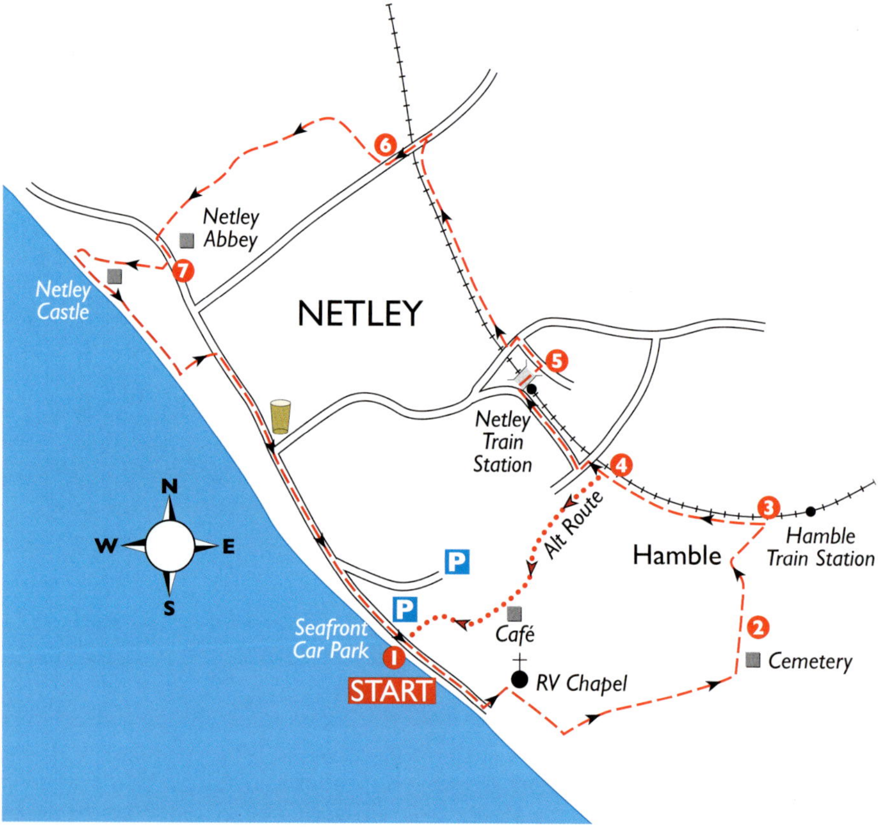

ground for the centre, signposts lead off to the left back to the **Royal Victoria Country Park** for those wanting a ***shorter route***.

❹ ***For the longer route***, continue straight on. Just before a railway bridge, turn left alongside houses and emerge onto a road with **The Sidings** trading estate on the right. Continue straight on for a few metres, then turn right onto a footpath on the right-hand side, soon walking beside the railway. The footpath turns into **The Badgers**, an access road for a housing estate. Continue straight on.

❺ At **Netley train station**, cross to Platform 2 (or if shut you can go round via **Station Road**) and out into the access road; turn left onto **St Mary's Road**, cross the main road and turn left. Just before the railway bridge, turn right onto a footpath back alongside the railway, with a housing estate on the right. Continue for just under half a mile, until the path bends to the right alongside

The ruins of Netley Abbey built in the 13th century.

a main road. Turn sharp left on the main road and, taking care on this short stretch, keep to the verges. Cross over the railway bridge and turn right just before **The Mill House** pub. Pass through a metal kissing gate into **Westwood Local Nature Reserve**.

6 Keep to the gravel path on the left, follow as it bends round to the left, and continue for about 300m through into woodlands. Continue straight on as a grass path turns off to the right. A few metres further on at a T-junction of paths, turn left; at a fork in paths take the left fork, and at a further fork, left again at an area of more open fields. Follow this path with horse paddocks to the right and a holly hedge on the left. The path bends to the left and exits onto a driveway via a metal kissing gate. Turn right and, at the main road, turn left, to **Netley Abbey** on the left-hand side.

7 After exploring the ruins, return to the road. Cross to the driveway of **Netley Castle** opposite and turn right through metal barriers into a park, with the tarmac path leading diagonally downhill towards Southampton Water. As the path nears the coastline, turn left across the grass to a footbridge across a small channel. Turn left onto a permissive footpath, enjoying views across the estuary with Netley Castle on the left. The path passes a community centre on the left and a small park. At the end of the park, turn left then turn right onto **Victoria Road**. Continue for half a mile through **Netley**, past the **Prince Consort** pub and sailing clubs to **The Hard** and the gates of **Royal Victoria Country Park**. Continue straight on for 500m to return to the **Seafront Car Park**.

What to look out for –

Royal Victoria Hospital Chapel and Military Cemetery

The Royal Victoria Hospital used to occupy much of the country park site. Opened in 1863 by Queen Victoria after the Crimean War, for the military, it closed in 1966 after a fire. The chapel is the only part of the building to remain. The hospital was over a quarter of a mile long, and wards faced the back of the hospital not out over the sea. Injured personnel had to be transferred from Southampton docks by train. The design attracted criticism from Florence Nightingale amongst others. The military cemetery contains over 4,000 graves, many from the Boer War and First World War.

View over Emsworth Harbour from the sea wall promenade.

16 Emsworth Harbour

4 miles / 6.4km

This figure-of-eight coastal walk from the historic fishing village of Emsworth takes in views across the Chichester Harbour Area of Outstanding Natural Beauty. Bracing but beautiful on a winter's day with a choice of warm pubs and cafés at the end. The walk starts with a promenade out into the harbour, and then along the shoreline to Warblington Church. The return route is known locally as the Coffin Walk. Before the church was built at Emsworth, coffins from the village had to be carried to Warblington Church. Please note this walk is tidal so you will need to check tide times, although there are shorter options.

winter

The Facts

Terrain Very flat. Part of the outward route is along a shingle beach inaccessible at high tide so check tide times. Return paths can be muddy.

Map OS Explorer OL 8 Chichester.

Starting point South Street car park (GR SU 749055).

How to get there & parking Emsworth is just off the A27 between Portsmouth and Chichester, accessed on the A259. Park at the pay and display car park on South Street. Emsworth railway station is less than half a mile from the starting point. **Sat nav** PO10 7EG.

Refreshments Several pubs, cafés and restaurants around South Street and High Street including the Blue Bell Inn ☎ 01243 373394. www.bluebellinnemsworth.co.uk.

The Walk

1 From the car park, exit onto **South Street** and turn right. Walk downhill and onto the quay. The footpath passes to the left-hand side of **Chichester Harbour Conservancy Office**, signposted **Wayfarer's Walk**. Follow a wide promenade on a sea wall out into the harbour, curving round to rejoin land at the southern end of **Bath Road**.

From the promenade enjoy views of Emsworth Mill Pond to the right, and out into the harbour towards Thorney Island to the left).

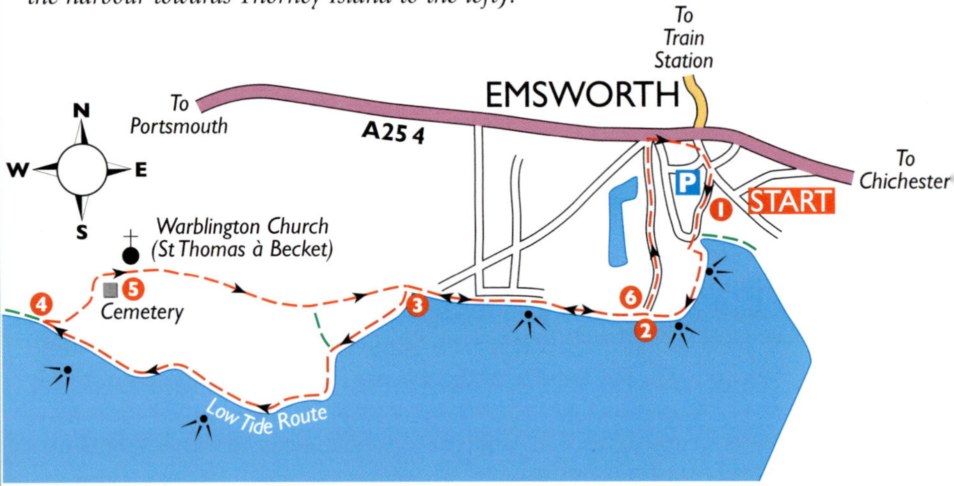

Walking along the shoreline path on a bracing winter's day.

2 Continue straight on past **Emsworth Sailing Club** on the left and through a short walkway to a concrete path along the shoreline. Follow this pathway for half a mile, in places open to vehicles along **Western Parade**. Pass **Kings Road**, **Beach Road** and **Warblington Road** to a further stretch of concrete shoreline path which soon drops onto shingle. From here the path is tidal. If it is approaching high tide you can shorten the walk and return to **Emsworth** via Point 6 from here.

3 If continuing, cross a small creek via a footbridge, with a low woodland (**Nore Barn Woods**) ahead, and here the path divides. Keep left along a footpath which follows the shoreline with the woods on your right. As the woodland ends, the main footpath turns right inland (a further alternative return route if tides are getting high). For the low tide route, drop onto the shingle and continue along the shoreline for three quarters of a mile as it curves round to the left, then the right, and yields views across to **Langstone** and **Hayling Island**.

4 Keep a look out for a metal kissing gate on the right-hand side in the fields just above the sea defences, and either climb up the shallow concrete sea defences to the gate, or walk a few hundred metres further, to where the footpath joins the shoreline, and double back. Cross the field diagonally to your right and enter into **Warblington Cemetery** via a kissing gate. Turn left, walking through the cemetery, then right (following footpath signs) and left again before a toilet block to a lane with **Warblington church** straight ahead.

5 Turn right along the lane with the churchyard on the left and the cemetery on the right and, as the lane turns left into a further section of the cemetery, continue straight on along a footpath, emerging into open fields. Continue straight on along a long field for 500m or so, keeping the hedge close on the right-hand side. Enter back into **Nore Barn Woods** through a kissing gate. Continue straight on, rejoining the shoreline path at point 3. Continue straight on, retracing your steps along the shoreline to Point 2 – Emsworth Sailing Club.

6 Turn left along **Bath Road** enjoying views of the mill pond on your right and continue to **Havant Road**. Turn right past **Bridgefoot Path**. Keep to the pavement and follow it diagonally right through bollards into **West Street**. Turn right into **High Street**, right again at **St Peter's Square** and continue along **South Street** back to the car park.

What to look out for –

Overwintering birds

Chichester Harbour Area of Outstanding Natural Beauty is not just deemed a special landscape, it is also internationally important for its birdlife, particularly its wading birds and wildfowl. Species like waders with their long beaks are able to probe in the rich mudflats within the harbour for food. Other species, like brent goose and wigeon, feed on plants and algae growing on the mud. Winter is a great time to see duck, geese and wading birds. Please remember not to disturb the birds, keep dogs under close control and stay to the paths.

Wintry views over the downs towards Plantation Hill.

17 Kingsclere and Watership Down

4 miles / 6.4km

With views of Watership Down and the dramatic scarp that it lies on, this walk on the edge of the North Wessex Downs Area of Outstanding Natural Beauty is uplifting in any winter weather. The walk starts in the pretty village of Kingsclere and circuits the southern edge of the village in gently rolling farmland with beautiful views of this scarp made famous by local author Richard Adams. This is also racehorse country and the walk passes gallops for the Park House Stables, owned by Clare Balding's family. Returning to the village, there are three warm pubs to choose from, and no fewer than 68 listed buildings.

winter

The Facts

Terrain Gently undulating; mainly on well surfaced footpaths, but muddy in patches.

Map OS Explorer 144 Basingstoke, Alton & Whitchurch.

Starting point The Fieldgate Centre (GR SU521587).

How to get there & parking Kingsclere lies just off the A339 between Basingstoke and Newbury. The free car park at the Fieldgate Centre is signposted from the Newbury road within the village. **Sat nav** RG20 5SQ.

Refreshments Several pubs and a café in the village including the Crown ☎ 01635 299500 www.thecrownkingsclere.co.uk, and Bel & The Dragon ☎ 01635 299342 www.belandthedragon-kingsclere.co.uk, plus a bar in the Fieldgate Centre.

Views across to Watership Down from Rectory Lane.

Kingsclere village.

The Walk

1 From the **Fieldgate Centre**, walk out of the car park back down towards **Foxs Lane**, cross the road onto the pavement and turn left. At the junction with **Newbury Road**, turn left and, just past **The Old House**, turn left again down **Frogs Hole**. Keeping to the left, follow a footpath up the side of a ditch, with a high fence to the right-hand side. Continue straight on along the side of the large field, right at the end (the official footpath goes diagonally across the field) and left into a second field, passing the barns of **Porch Farm** on the right-hand side. Just past the barns, turn right, then left, skirting the edge of a third field. Pass through a gap in the hedge and down a couple of steps onto a sunken path and turn left. Continue straight on to **Ecchinswell Road**.

2 Turn right along this rural road and continue for 200m. Turn left at a footpath sign along a farm track and continue to a large barn. Turn left at the barn, keeping the field boundary to your left-hand side, and now with views across to the scarp on your right-hand side and **Watership Down** (see box below). Continue straight on, passing through a gap in the hedge to a second field and continue down through a small gate onto **Foxs Lane**.

3 Turn right then immediately left onto **Bear Hill**, passing houses to the right and left and, at the bottom of the hill at a triangle of land and a fork in the

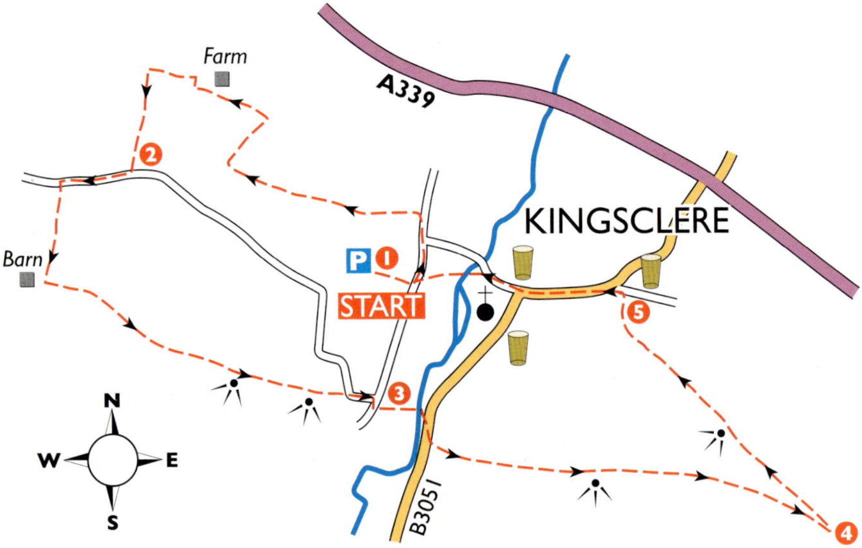

road, take the right-hand fork, and cross over the road to a wide bridleway opposite, **Hollowshot Lane**. Continue straight on as it goes from a wide track to a wooded footpath, enjoying views across to the **Park House Stables**, racehorse gallops and the downland scarp.

Park House Stables is owned by Andrew Balding. He and his sister, TV presenter Clare, grew up here. If you are lucky you might see a future race winner being exercised on the gallops.

4 After just under a mile in total, climbing steadily, the path reaches a distinct fork and meeting of paths. Turn sharp left, uphill, along **Rectory Lane**, a wide track with high hedges on both sides and occasional glimpses back to the scarp. Continue straight on as the path reaches the crest of the rise and goes back down the other side before becoming a tarmac road, **The Dell**. Continue straight on to the junction with **Basingstoke Road** and turn left.

5 Passing the **George and Horn** pub on the right and fire station on the left, join **George Street** and continue straight on down this road to the church and village centre. After suitable refreshments, continue straight on past the church on the left and the **Crown** pub on the right. At **Brewery Cottage**, leave the main road and take the left-hand road (entrance closed to cars), **Popes Hill**. At the top of the road, turn left and right into **Field Gate Drive**.

What to look out for –

Watership Down

Watership Down is a hill or down on a much longer chalk scarp feature. It is the furthest part of the scarp seen here covered in snow. It was made famous in Richard Adam's 1972 book about a fictional group of rabbits including Hazel, Fiver and Bigwig as they flee their warren in search of a new home and, after many adventures, settle at Watership Down. Adams described the area as: "High, lonely hills, where the wind and the sound carry and the ground's as dry as straw in a barn".

Views across the South Downs from Charlton Down.

18 Chalton Down and St Hubert's Church

5.5 miles / 8.8km

This walk on the Hampshire-Sussex border has an archaeological flavour and winter is the best time to be able to see sites and monuments. Starting with a climb up to Chalton Down in the South Downs National Park, the bowl barrow on top of the hill reminds us of just how long people have been using this landscape. Views can be had to Windmill Hill, Compton Down and even across to Portsmouth and Portsdown Hill on a clear day. The route returns via Finchdean and the Staunton Way, passing the atmospheric St Hubert's Church, surrounded by fields. A stiff climb back up Chalton Down ends at the Red Lion in Chalton, one of the oldest pubs in Hampshire. This is a robust winter walk, great for burning off the excesses of Christmas.

The Facts

Terrain One steep climb and some moderate ascents and descents on rural footpaths and rural roads; can be muddy.

Map OS Explorer OL 8 Chichester.

Starting point Chalton village car park (GR SU732160).

How to get there & parking Chalton is just off the A3, signposted Chalton and Clanfield. Follow signs to Butser Ancient Farm, and then continue straight on to the village. There is a free car park next to the Red Lion pub. **Sat nav** PO8 0BG.

Refreshments The Red Lion, Chalton ☎ 023 9259 2246 www.redlionchalton.co.uk, and the George, Finchdean ☎ 023 9241 2257 www.thegeorgefinchdean.co.uk, both en route.

winter

The Walk

1 Exit the car park using the path on the left-hand side, and cross the road to the church. Enter through the gates and pass the church to a wooden gate at the rear of the churchyard. Pass through this wooden gate to a kissing gate, and follow the path round to the left following the hedge-line. Cross a farm track to a further kissing gate onto **Chalton Down**. Here there is a choice of three paths leading across the large arable field. Take the right-hand path signposted **Staunton Way**, which leads diagonally up the arable field to a kissing gate. Continue straight on up the crest of the hill across a second arable field. The top of the hill is marked by a grassy area, with a round barrow forming a prominent feature.

This is a bowl barrow thought to date from the late Neolithic or Bronze Age (see box below).

2 Continue straight on, pass through a kissing gate, and straight across the field opposite, enjoying views down to **St Hubert's Church**. Look out for a kissing gate on the left three quarters of the way down the field; pass through and continue straight on, keeping to the field boundary and skirting a copse to a junction of four crossing paths in front of another copse.

This is the area where a Saxon village was found, high on the hilltop.

3 Continue straight on, keeping the wooded field boundary to the right. The path bends to the left and you then start descending. At a further copse, look out for a footpath signpost and turn right along an unsurfaced farm track. Ignore

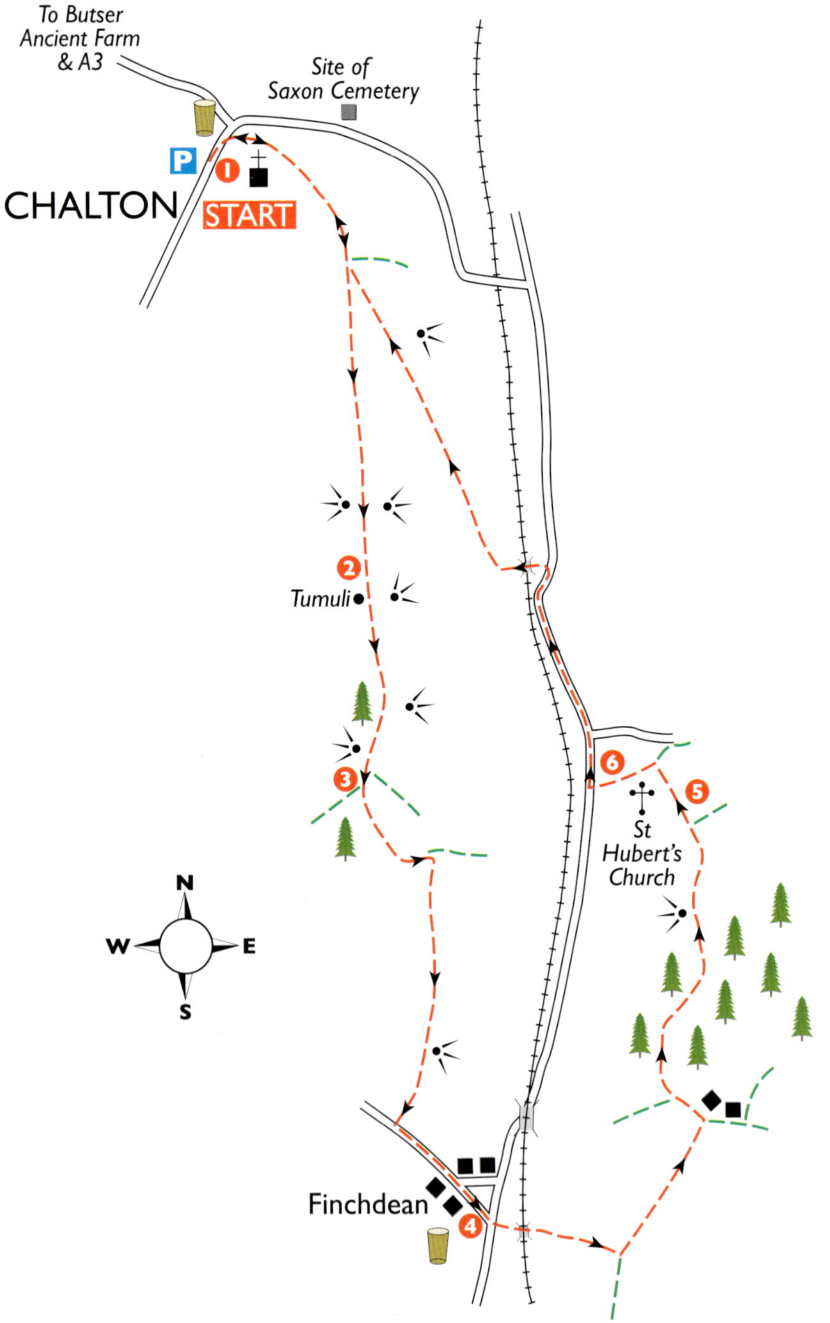
To Butser
Ancient Farm
& A3
Site of
Saxon Cemetery
CHALTON
START
Tumuli
St
Hubert's
Church
N
W
E
S
Finchdean

St Hubert's church surrounded by fields.

the path downhill to the left, and continue straight on into an arable field, with the hedgerow to your right, and descend to **Finchdean**. At the bottom of the hill, turn left, staying in the field, and continue to a gap in the hedge to a fork of two rural lanes. Take the right-hand fork to find the village green. Cross the road to the pub and turn right.

4 At the corner of the pub car park closest to the road, turn left just before the large farm gate over a stile into a pathway between hedges, following the **Staunton Way**. Pass under the railway bridge and out into an open arable field. Continue straight on across the field, uphill and at a slight diagonal angle aiming towards the corner of a hedgerow with trees. Continue straight on with the hedgerow to your left to a well-surfaced farm access lane. Turn left here, passing through a copse and back out into open grazed pasture fields.

5 Just before two farm dwellings, take the left-hand fork in lanes, passing a farm cottage on the right. As the driveway turns right, continue along a grassy path to a kissing gate. Cross the corner of the field to a stile, and walk straight on across the next field to the woodland ahead. Continue along the Staunton Way through the woodland for around 500m descending to views of **Old Idsworth Garden**. Pass through a kissing gate and keep to the field boundary, crossing to a stile straight ahead. Cross the corner of a field to a metal kissing gate on the right and continue along the arable field, with the hedgerow to your left. After 250m or so, turn left through a kissing gate to a path leading down to explore **St Hubert's Church**.

This church was built in the 11th century by Earl Godwin, father of King Harold. It originally served a small village, thought to have become deserted in the 1300s, possibly after an outbreak of the plague.

6 From the church, continue straight down to **Finchdean Road** and turn right, signposted to **Chalton**. After 500m, as the road bends sharply to the right, look out for a stile on the left-hand side and cross towards the railway line. Turn right, following the railway for a few metres and turn left under a railway bridge. Continue straight on up the arable field, and turn right along a path through scrub, skirting the hillside. Pass through a kissing gate to re-enter **Chalton Down** and start the climb up the side of the down. Cross a kissing gate back into an arable field and continue straight on, diagonally climbing the crest of the hill. Pass through a gap in the hedge to a second arable field, over the hill and back to the kissing gate to pick up the pathway down to the church, pub and car park.

What to look out for –

Round Barrows, Chalton Down

The strange mound by the footpath is one of three archaeological remnants of bowl barrows, or round barrows. These are a funerary monument dating from the late Neolithic or Bronze Age (2400-1500 BC). These earthen or rubble mounds covered burials, often in prominent locations, and the evidence of multiple mounds suggests that the barrow was part of a larger cemetery site, and a major focus of ritual activity during the later prehistoric period. Jumping forward in time, archaeologists also found a Saxon cemetery in Chalton, and a village of at least 61 homes on Chalton Down (Point 3, at the junction of paths). These finds remind us of just how long people have been living in, using and moving through the same land that we see today.

Walking up towards the Harrow Way from Overton Mill.

19 Overton

5 miles / 8km

This walk passes Overton Mill, which produces bank notes and security papers for over 150 countries, including the Bank of England, and then joins the Harrow Way, a wooded drovers' route and ancient track with views across the chalk downs of the North Wessex Downs Area of Outstanding Natural Beauty. Returning to Overton, the route tracks the River Test, a clear chalk stream famed for its trout fishing and protected for its importance to wildlife. There are two further picturesque old mills along the route and the historic village of Overton to explore with four pubs providing cheer on a cold winter day. Visitors can also make a day of it by visiting Laverstoke Mill, now the Bombay Sapphire Distillery.

The Facts

Terrain An undulating walk with some gentle climbs and descents. Mainly well-surfaced paths but can be muddy in places.

Map OS Explorer 144 Basingstoke, Alton & Whitchurch.

Starting point Overton train station (GR SU518508).

How to get there & parking Overton lies to the west of Basingstoke on the B3400, accessible from the M3 via Basingstoke or the A34 via Whitchurch. Regular trains from London/Basingstoke and Andover. There is free parking at the station or spaces in the centre of Overton. **Sat nav** RG25 3JG.

Refreshments Overton boasts four pubs and a café, including the Red Lion ☎ 01256 773363 www.redlion-overton.co.uk. There is also a bar during visitor centre opening hours at the Bombay Sapphire Distillery at Laverstoke. ☎ 01256 890090.

The Walk

1 From Platform 1 of the station, turn right through the grey gate onto a permissive footpath alongside the **De La Rue Overton Mill** factory [alternative route if needed via **Station Approach**, **Kingsdown Lane** and **Papermill Lane**]. After a few hundred metres, this path comes out at the main entrance. Turn left, passing a large green gate, the security office and a further green gate, onto a path running alongside the boundary fence with the staff car park on your right, signposted as a byway. Keep walking uphill, leaving the large mill site behind, and continue straight on over the hill into a dip and back up, with the **Harrow Way** now visible ahead.

2 At a junction of paths, turn left onto the Harrow Way. Continue straight on to **Kingsclere Road**, and, taking care, cross this fast country road to a byway sign slightly to the right. Continue along this wooded path for just over a mile, passing a crossing footpath, a byway and a footpath to the left. Watch out for a further crossing pathway, signposted **Jack Wills Lane**, named after a local policeman.

3 Turn left and continue straight down this track for three quarters of a mile, crossing the railway line just over halfway. At a large house, turn left onto a surfaced vehicle track and continue for a further three quarters of

Try telling the time the old-fashioned way using Overton's human sundial.

of a mile in total, following the **River Test**, and then becoming a tarmac road.

Look out for Southington Mill on the right-hand side.

4 At a junction of roads, turn right down **Court Drove** and then right onto **Bridge Street**. Turn left onto **High Street** to reach the centre of historic **Overton**. After exploring the village and finding suitable refreshment, turn left onto **Kingsclere Road** and, climbing slightly here, pass the church, stopping to explore if time allows, and the nature garden just after the church with a 'human sundial'.

5 After passing allotments on the right, turn right down the first signposted footpath you come to, a surfaced track again following the route of the River Test and an important wildlife area known as **Flashetts**. Pass **Flashetts House** on the left and continue along the path, now narrower alongside the Test, and soon opening up to views of **Quidhampton Mill** on the right. Cross a small footbridge onto **Station Road**. Turn left and follow Station Road back up to the station.

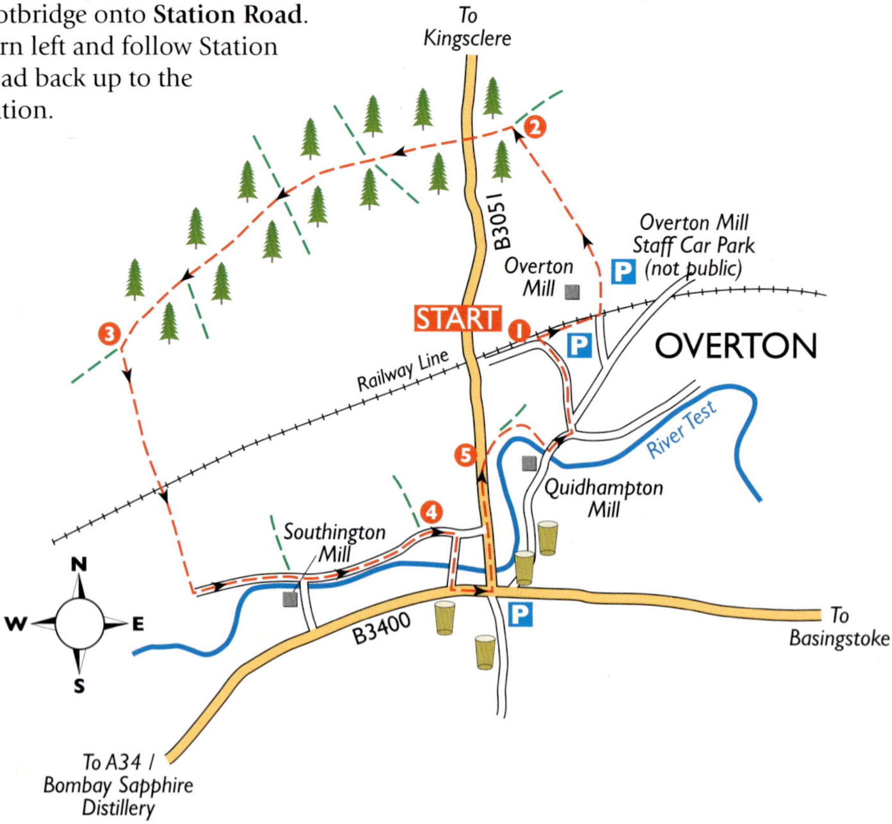

What to look out for –

Historic mills

Overton has been at the heart of specialist paper-making since the 18th century, with two paper mill sites along the Test Valley, as well as fulling mills and corn mills such as the 18th-century Southington Mill and the 17th- and 18th-century Quidhampton Mill, both on the route and now private dwellings. The De La Rue site is now industrial and makes banknotes and other high-security paper for governments around the world, whilst the historic Laverstoke paper mill further towards Whitchurch now hosts Bombay Sapphire's visitor centre. Whitchurch Silk Mill also hosts a popular visitor centre.

The colours of the New Forest are still beautiful on a rainy day along the Holmsley Railway Line.

20 Burley and the Holmsley Railway Line

3.5 miles / 5.6km

Starting in the pretty village of Burley in the New Forest National Park, this walk climbs from the village and onto a heathland plateau with great views from the ridge. You will then descend to an old railway, once part of the Southampton to Dorchester line which closed in 1964. From the remnants of the railway line's Greenberry Bridge there is a climb back up to the plateau and into Burley. A family-friendly walk ideal for grey winter days with warm cafés and pubs awaiting your return.

The Walk

1 From the village car park, walk back onto **Chapel Lane**, turn right, pass the **Queens Head** pub and cross the road when safe to do so. Turn left between the two gift shops onto a footpath leading up into woodland. Pass through

Burley and the Holmsley Railway Line

The Facts

Terrain Undulating with some short but steep climbs and descents; mainly on clearly defined pathways but likely to be muddy in places, especially after rain.

Map OS Explorer OL 22 New Forest.

Starting point The centre of Burley village (GR SU 212031).

How to get there & parking Burley lies between Ringwood and Lyndhurst, a few minutes' drive from either the A35 or A31 and signposted from both roads. There is a pay and display car park in the centre of the village. Alternative parking at Forestry Commission sites Burley and Burley Cricket. **Sat nav** BH24 4AA.

Refreshments Various options in Burley, including the Burley Inn ☎ 01425 403448 www.theburleyinn.co.uk, and the Old Farmhouse Restaurant and Tea Rooms ☎ 01425 402218 www.oldfarmhouseinburley.co.uk.

Crossing Holmsley Bog on a raised pathway.

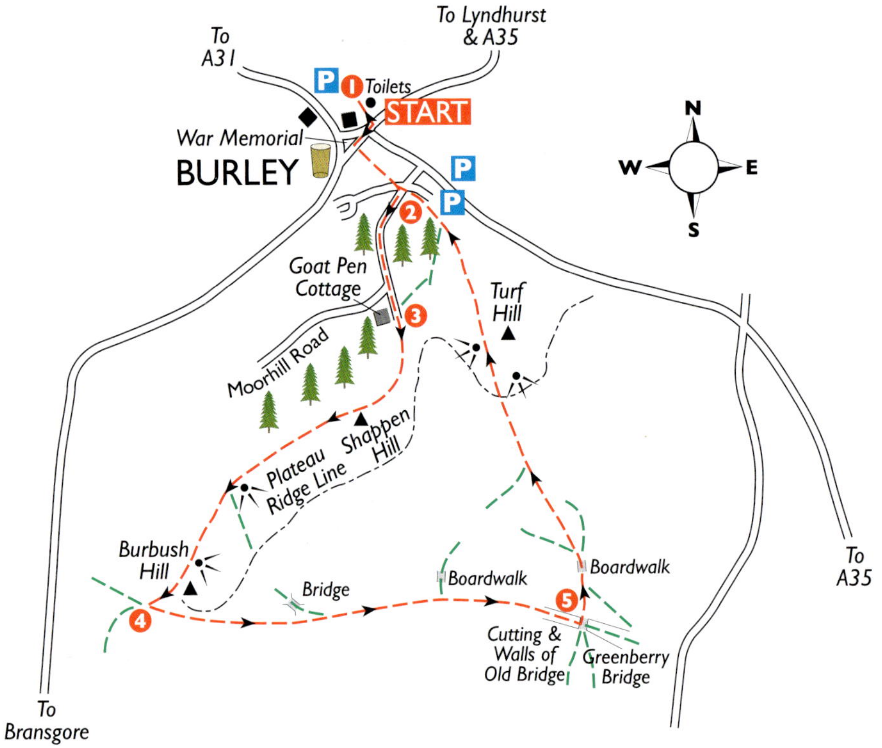

a wooden barrier. The path emerges onto a gravel drive and a crossroads of vehicle access tracks.

2 Take the third driveway on the right, a tarmac access lane signposted **Moorhill House Hotel**. Continue down the wooded lane for 300m or so, then take a left-hand fork onto an unsurfaced vehicle track signposted **Goat Pen Cottage**.

3 At the corner of the cottage, continue straight ahead onto the heath past four short posts. The path is undefined here. Aim to the left of the woodland and pick up a defined gravel track uphill onto **Shappen Hill** and a ridgeline with clear views across the valley to the left. Continue along this path for three quarters of a mile, as it undulates into a dip, up onto **Burbush Hill** and down more steeply to join an old railway line.

4 Turn left and follow the railway line for a mile, passing a path and a bridge on the left, a further path and boardwalk on the left. The old railway line enters into a cutting.

5 Turn left at an old brick structure, formerly **Greenberry Bridge** onto a gravel pathway downhill slightly, crossing **Holmsley Bog** on a raised pathway, then up onto the heath. Follow this gravel path up **Turf Hill** and back onto the plateau. The path emerges at **Burley car park**. Continue straight on onto a woodland track. This brings you back out at Point 2. Continue straight on along the woodland path to return to **Burley**.

What to look out for –

New Forest ponies

New Forest ponies are descended from wild ponies, and recognised as a distinct breed, but they are not wild animals. All of them are owned by 'commoners', local people who have rights over the forest such as the right to graze animals freely. The heathland around Burley is very important for wildlife and grazing by the ponies helps to maintain this unique landscape. New Forest ponies have evolved to be able to eat coarse, prickly vegetation, including gorse and holly. Do be careful driving on New Forest roads to help protect the ponies and please don't feed them.